PRIORITIES FOR ACTION: FINAL REPORT OF THE CARNEGIE COMMISSION ON HIGHER EDUCATION

WITH TECHNICAL NOTES AND APPENDIXES

McGRAW-HILL BOOK COMPANY
New York   St. Louis   San Francisco   Düsseldorf
London   Sydney   Toronto   Mexico   Panama
Johannesburg   Kuala Lumpur   Montreal
New Delhi   São Paulo   Singapore

Library of Congress Cataloging in Publication Data
Carnegie Commission on Higher Education.
Priorities for action.
Bibliography: p.
1. Education, Higher—United States—History.
I.   Title.
LA227.3.C38   1973   378.73   73-15714
ISBN 0-07-010072-1 (Soft cover)
ISBN 0-07-010104-3 (Hard cover)

This book was set in Claro by University Graphics, Inc.
It was printed and bound by The Maple Press Company.
The designer was Edward Butler.
The editors were Terry Y. Allen, Michael Hennelly, Janine Parson,
and Nancy Tressel.
Bill Greenwood supervised the production.

When the wheel [of education] has once been set in motion, the speed is always increasing . . .

Dialogues of Plato
(Jowett, vol. 3)

. . . for everything you gain, you lose something else.

Emerson,
Essays

Observe degree, priority and place . . .

Ulysses speaks,
Troilus and Cressida, Shakespeare

The task of a university is the creation of the future, so far as rational thought and civilized modes of appreciation can affect the issue.

Alfred North Whitehead,
Modes of Thought

CONTENTS

market   Collective bargaining   Women's liberation movement   Rising interest in the welfare of the total postsecondary age group   The shift of initiative to the states   New enrollment patterns   New mentalities   Absorption of women and minorities

FOREWORD

The Carnegie Commission on Higher Education was established in 1967 by The Carnegie Foundation for the Advancement of Teaching. It was asked to study and to make recommendations about higher education for the 1970s and ahead to the year 2000.

The Commission has issued 21 special reports (see Appendix A for a chronological listing and Appendix G for the table of contents of each of the reports of the Commission) and has sponsored a series of special studies which will have appeared in a total of around 80 publications and issued some 30 reprints (see Appendix B for chronological listings of sponsored studies, technical reports, and reprints).

The Commission has met on 33 occasions in 26 different cities for a total of 77 days (see Appendix C for a list of dates and locations). The attendance of members at meetings has been remarkable: two members missed no meetings; one missed only one meeting; and five missed three or fewer meetings. Average attendance has been 15 out of the 18 members resident in the United States. Each special report was discussed in at least three meetings and some in as many as eight meetings; and each member present participated in the discussion of each report on each agenda.

The Commission had the opportunity to meet with several hundred leaders of higher education as it held its meetings in some 21 states, the District of Columbia, and Puerto Rico; and a number of these leaders were our gracious hosts.

Many persons have contributed to the work of the Commission, including the authors of sponsored studies and of technical reports, and the advisors on several of the special reports. Their contributions were absolutely essential to the work of the Commission.

The staff has been of fundamental importance to the efforts of the Commission, and a deep debt of gratitude is due to its members. We are particularly mindful of the contributions of Associate Directors Margaret S. Gordon, Virginia Smith, and Verne Stadtman. (Appendix D sets forth the names of staff members who served part time or full time for half the life of the Commission or more, with their final titles.)

Throughout its deliberations the Commission has had the great advantage of the good advice and most helpful criticisms of the members of the Technical Advisory Committee, which discussed each of the reports of the Commission in draft form. No member of this Committee could agree with all of our reports in full—in fact, several had basic objections to aspects of several reports—but all members contributed greatly to an understanding of the issues and to the exploration of possible solutions to problems. (For the members of this Committee, with dates of their service, see Appendix E.)

The Commission appreciates the continuing support of The Carnegie Foundation for the Advancement of Teaching, which was given without any effort to influence the recommendations of the Commission; and it has gained greatly from the advice and the devoted attendance at Commission meetings of senior members of the staff of the Carnegie Corporation: Alan Pifer, president; David Z. Robinson, vice-president; E. Alden Dunham, executive associate; and Richard H. Sullivan, assistant to the president. (For a discussion of the Commission from the point of view of The Carnegie Foundation for the Advancement of Teaching, see Appendix F.)

The tolerance of the higher education community of the United States has been quite remarkable, for the Commission, in speaking *about* higher education, did not, in major instances, speak on policy, as have those who could speak *for* higher education.

The interest in the work of the Commission by public officials and legislators with responsibility for higher education affairs, and their willingness to give consideration to the Commission— and even put into application its recommendations—has been most gratifying.

The press and the information media generally have been most generous and exceedingly fair in the presentation of the Commission's proposals.

The McGraw-Hill Book Company has been both effective and considerate in its publication of Commission reports and studies, and several of its officials have contributed great talent and much time. We particularly appreciate the contributions made by Dan Lacy, senior vice-president; Thomas H. Quinn, publisher, Scholarly Books Division; Nancy Tressel, editor, Scholarly Books Division; Morrie Helitzer, vice-president public affairs; Victor de Keyserling, director of public information and publicity, and the dedicated and exceptional staff of the Editing Services department.

The Educational Testing Service, through its Berkeley Office, has been a model landlord, providing space and services with the best of goodwill.

The Library of the University of California at Berkeley has endured with stoic restraint innumerable requests for books and periodicals, and out of its vast resources has met these requests in a most generous manner.

The Ford Foundation has joined with us on several projects without hesitation, with good counsel and needed funds, and with an excellent spirit of cooperation; and the Commonwealth Fund similarly cooperated in one major project in the health care field.

The Office of Education helped finance most generously a major survey project that was conducted jointly with the American Council on Education; the Commission is indebted to both of these organizations. Martin Trow and Joseph Zelan, with the participation of the Survey Research Center of the University of California at Berkeley, conducted this survey with great talent and persistence.

Above all, each of us owes an immense debt of gratitude to The Carnegie Foundation for the Advancement of Teaching, in general, and to Alan Pifer, in particular, for giving us this unique opportunity to study and to discuss and to make recommendations on the welfare of higher education. We have gained more personally in understanding and in friendships than we have been able to contribute in return.

ERIC ASHBY
The Master
Clare College
Cambridge, England

RALPH M. BESSE
Partner
Squire, Sanders & Dempsey
* Counsellors at Law*

JOSEPH P. COSAND
Professor of Education and
* Director*
Center for Higher Education
University of Michigan

WILLIAM FRIDAY
President
University of North Carolina

THE HONORABLE PATRICIA
ROBERTS HARRIS
Partner
Fried, Frank, Harris, Shriver &
* Kampelman, Attorneys*

DAVID D. HENRY
President Emeritus
Distinguished Professor of Higher
* Education*
University of Illinois

PRIORITIES FOR ACTION: FINAL REPORT OF THE CARNEGIE COMMISSION ON HIGHER EDUCATION

THE CURRENT STAGE OF DEVELOPMENT

FROM GOLDEN AGE TO TIME OF TROUBLES

CHAPTER

The extension of formal education into more and more of the lives of more and more of the people has been one of the great social developments in the United States, and the world, in recent centuries. The "Educational" Revolution stands along with the "Industrial" and the "Democratic" revolutions (Parsons, 1971) as a major force in transforming the life of modern man in all Western societies, and in most others as well. The educational revolution supports both the technological base of the industrial revolution and the humanitarian base of the democratic revolution; and it is inseparable from both of them.

The United States has taken the lead historically in this educational revolution, starting earlier and advancing further than other nations. Today nearly 20 percent of an average lifetime in the United States is spent in substantial attention to formal education—12.6 years out of 71, and the percentage has risen rapidly over the past century (see Chart 1, page 10). If all costs of formal education in all institutions are added up and forgone earnings are included, about one-eighth of our national productive effort is spent on formal education (Machlup, 1962).

We have been moving toward the age of the "Learning Society"[1] (Hutchins, 1968) in the sense that nearly every person beyond early childhood would come to have formal educational opportunities available in nearly every circumstance of life, and many, if not most, would avail themselves of these opportunities; that learning would be at or near the center of activity for substantial portions of most individual lives and of many of the functions of society.

Yet education in the United States—primary, secondary, and higher education—is in grave trouble. Higher education, after a period of 20 years following World War II when it attained its greatest glory through notable achievements in scientific research and through expansion to serve huge additional numbers of students, now faces several intense crises suddenly and almost all at once. Sustained growth in effort and in attainments has given way to doubts and to difficulties.

The "Educational" Revolution stands along with the "Industrial" and the "Democratic" revolutions as a major force in transforming the life of modern man in all Western societies, and in most others as well.

THE POLITICAL CRISIS

In recent times, students and faculty members in unprecedented numbers have engaged in political activity, some of it illegal, against dominant policies and institutions in the sur-

Yet education in the United States—primary, secondary, and higher education—is in grave trouble.

[1] We define "learning," however, more broadly than does Hutchins to include technical training and other quasi-academic and nonacademic programs.

rounding society. Campuses have been torn apart; relations with external groups seriously damaged. Dissent is an essential aspect of academic life and there was much to dissent about; but the disruption was excessive. Today an eerie quietude has descended on the campus.

But higher education has not yet made up its collective mind about how it should and will conduct itself vis-à-vis the political arena, and it remains to be seen whether it will want to make up its mind and be able to do so; the public at large has not yet renewed its full faith in higher education—once bitten, it is still shy; and new confrontations on campus and off are just as possible in the future as the potentialities for such future confrontations are blindly ignored in the present. The "adversary culture," or cultures, so well developed on so many campuses, almost certainly will confront the "bedrock culture" of so much of the surrounding society on new, just as it has on old, occasions.

THE FINANCIAL DEPRESSION

Institutions of higher education escaped their traditional genteel poverty after World War II; they even became newly prosperous. But a "new depression" has quickly followed the newfound prosperity, and it is likely to be more enduring—higher education has moved from genteel poverty to genteel poverty in one generation. It is undoubtedly better to have prospered and to have lost than never to have prospered at all, but the adjustment to the new depression is more difficult than was the adjustment to the new prosperity.

THE DEMOGRAPHIC CHANGE

Higher education has been a growth segment of American society since 1636. It is no longer. Enrollments of "traditional" students will most likely decline on established campuses in the 1980s, and subsequently advance more with, than so rapidly ahead of, the growth of the American population. This new stage of development comes as a great shock, a great change of life, and creates many new problems. It marks a first descent into a strange world where future prospects are no longer thought to be limitless.

THE ADJUSTMENT TO UNIVERSAL ACCESS

Three periods of basic transformation potentially confront the development of any system of higher education. The first such period comes with the movement from (1) elite (or restricted) to mass higher education, from service for the few to service for the many. This transition in the United States began with the land-grant movement after the Civil War and reached its climax with the G.I. rush after World War II. Shortly on its heels came the transition from (2) mass higher education to universal-access higher education in the 1960s and continuing into the 1970s. The universal-access stage, in turn, has two subperiods: first, universal access for members of the "college-age" population, and second, universal access for persons of all ages. The third transformation, if it ever comes, which we hope it will not, would take the form of (3) universal or nearly universal attendance in college, rather than universal access.[2] The current transition to universal access to college involves the guarantee of a place for every high school student who wishes to enter higher education, the introduction of more remedial work, the adaptation to the interests of new groups of students regardless of age, the substantial increase in total costs, and the augmentation of public interest and control. It is a transformation of fundamental, historic proportions.

[2] We do expect, however, in the future, universal or nearly universal attendance in some form of "postsecondary education," including "further education," at some point in life, but not necessarily in the traditional colleges that constitute "higher education." The stages of development as we see them are: (1) elite higher education, (2) mass higher education, (3) universal-access higher education, first, for the college-age group and, then, for persons of all ages, and (4) universal attendance (or nearly universal attendance) in some form of postsecondary education. Stage (4) might be, as an alternative, universal attendance in higher education, but we shall set forth later why we believe this would be an unwise development. The terms we use are defined as follows: "higher education" as academic or occupational programs on a college or university campus or in campus-substitute institutions such as the "open university"; "further education" as quasi-academic and nonacademic programs involved in training specific skills through industry, the military, and other institutions; "postsecondary" (or "tertiary") education as including both higher and further education. "Traditional" students we define as full-time students attending courses aimed at an academic degree; and "nontraditional" students as part-time students or non-degree-credit students or both. The "knowledge sector" of society includes all formal education, including primary and secondary schools, as well as postsecondary education, and all other elements which produce and distribute information, such as the media, research and development, the computer industry, and much else.

THE LABOR MARKET TRANSFORMATION

Appropriate jobs for college graduates were taken for granted, except in deep depressions, until about 1968. Now a new long-term situation has developed. Job prospects for college graduates, we believe, will be generally better than in 1968 to 1973, as far as we can see ahead, but it seems likely that the absorption ability of the labor market for some years in the future—especially for some occupations—will fall below the output rate of college graduates by significant, though not by overwhelming, margins. College capacity to train students has expanded more rapidly, particularly in the 1960s when it more than doubled, than the capacity of the economy to provide places for graduates at the level of their training.

THE EXPANSION OF EXPECTATIONS WHEN HIGHER EDUCATION IS APPROACHING A "STATIONARY STATE"

Women and members of minority groups have greatly increased their hopes for faculty positions at a time when the rate of new hires is declining rapidly.

THE CRISIS OF CONFIDENCE

These other crises have caused a crisis of confidence among faculty members, administrators, trustees, public officials with responsibility for higher education, and among the public at large. The "confidence ranking" of many major American institutions has fallen significantly in recent times, according to a Harris poll, but that of "education" somewhat more than the average (see Appendix Table 1). There has been a basic erosion of affection for and interest in education, including higher education. A sense of confidence once lost is not easily restored.

A lack of confidence now exists in what is being done, in conceptions of what should be done, in the processes for making changes. This lack of confidence weakens administrative leadership on campus.

A traumatic loss of a sense of assured progress, of the inevitability of a better future, has occurred.

A traumatic loss of a sense of assured progress, of the inevitability of a better future, has occurred. Instead there has developed more of a nostalgia for a Paradise Lost. The tone of so much academic thought is now more an attitude of how to hold on to as much of the past as possible—or even to retrieve lost aspects of it—rather than of how to confront the future directly; of how to avoid change, since most possible changes are thought to be unfavorable or even disastrous, rather than of how to plan and support constructive new developments. The prevalent attitude is more to look back with longing than to look ahead with hope—the situation may be bad but it cannot be improved; the Golden Age of the past is more attractive than any conceivable prospects for the future. The faith in a future that would surpass the present sustained a century of progress in higher education—from the end of the Civil War up to the time of the Vietnam War—but now no longer. It should be noted, however, that differing segments of higher education are differently affected by this malaise—the public community colleges, in particular, have almost entirely escaped it; private colleges and elite universities, both public and private, may be most affected.

This view that the Golden Age of higher education lies more in the past than in the future parallels, but exceeds, that of the nation at large. The social idealism and social optimism that characterized the New Deal and the period following World War II have given way to cynicism and to pessimism. This idealism and optimism led to substantial accomplishments. Where may cynicism and pessimism, if long continued, lead?

THE NEW RAILROAD INDUSTRY?

Will higher education, weighted down by these and other crises, follow the course of the railroad industry?

Will higher education, weighted down by these and other crises, follow the course of the railroad industry? Both have been great sources of national growth—the railroad industry in the second half of the nineteenth century, and higher education particularly in the middle of the twentieth century. The railroad industry, in the face of new competitors arising out of new technologies and new public tastes, and burdened by old mentalities, old practices, old and rigid operating rules, an older and aging labor force, and restrictive government controls has declined greatly in dynamism and influence; it has become a largely spent force in terms of additional national growth. The transportation segment of the economy kept on growing, but the railroad industry declined within it.

Will higher education follow a similar course and for much the same reasons? Will it decline even as postsecondary education, which includes potentially fast-growing further education, expands; and even as the still larger knowledge sector of society grows? New competitors and new technologies also now challenge higher education, and new tastes and patterns for obtaining tertiary education likewise are emerging.

Similarities do exist between the historical courses of higher education and of the railroad industry, but there are major dissimilarities as well. One dissimilarity—and we consider it fundamental—is that the railroad industry approached its decline and subsequent stagnation over a long period of time and as a result of long-term factors. The new depression in higher education is a sudden affair and can be explained, in substantial part, by sudden developments rather than simply by forces necessarily leading to a long downward trend into stagnation. It is our opinion that higher education is now more involved in a medium-term "time of troubles," lasting for perhaps a decade or two, rather than in a permanent reduction of essentiality and vitality; that it is experiencing more a temporary pause in its development than the start of a long-term secular decline; that it will regain forward momentum but most probably not at the rate of the post-World War II period, which was most unusual in its combination of expansive forces:

- The "wheel" of education has moved forward, but now faster and now slower, since the time of Plato, although at a particularly rapid rate in recent decades in the United States. Greater wealth makes possible still further forward momentum, and the desires of individuals and of society make it necessary. (See Chart 2, and also Appendix Table 2 and Appendix Chart 1.)

- New types of students are likely to be brought into higher education, particularly adults seeking "recurrent" education; and standard enrollments of college-age students may start rising again in the 1990s after the decline in the 1980s.

- University research, which expanded so greatly after World War II, is likely to be needed perhaps even more in the future. Ever greater problems will need solutions, and the university continues to be a most productive source of both basic and applied research. And service follows research.

The secular trends in requirements for both instruction and research at the highest levels are most likely to be upward in direction. The secular trends in requirements for both instruction and research at the highest levels are most likely to be upward in direction. These secular tendencies, which we do not believe will be reversed, create a base from which higher education can resume its forward momentum, but they do not, of course, guarantee this result. Higher education must also act in ways that benefit from and encourage these basic trends, and must help solve other problems along the way such as the political, financial, and confidence crises noted earlier.

The winds of rapidly rising enrollments, of relatively easy money, of fantastic expansion of research activity have subsided. Stagnation, however, is not likely and certainly not inevitable. Continuation of all the current crises is not inescapable. We believe that higher education itself, and those interested in and responsible for its welfare in the larger society, can take actions which will reduce the gravity of at least some of the crises. We believe that such actions are not only possible but also imperative.

We do not believe higher education will decline, and we are convinced that it would be a tragedy for the nation if it did.

We do not believe higher education will decline, and we are convinced that it would be a tragedy for the nation if it did. We end our six years of study of higher education, in the time of its greatest trauma of self-doubt, with faith in its potential continued vitality and with a deepened belief in its essential value to American society.

CHART 1 Average years* spent in formal education

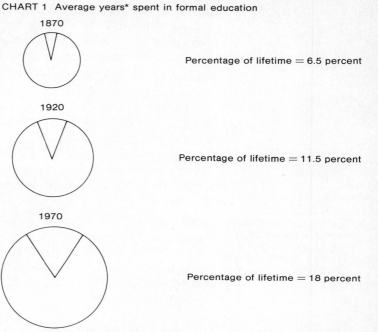

1870

Percentage of lifetime = 6.5 percent

1920

Percentage of lifetime = 11.5 percent

1970

Percentage of lifetime = 18 percent

*Adjusted for greater absenteeism and shorter school years in 1870 and 1920 than in 1970.

NOTE: Circumference is proportional to life expectation at birth: 41 years in 1870, 54 years in 1920, and 71 years in 1970.

CHART 2   Selected measures of educational attainment of the population 25 years old and over, 1910–2000

Percentage of population with:

☐ College 4 or more years

▨ College 1–3 years

▧ High School 4 years

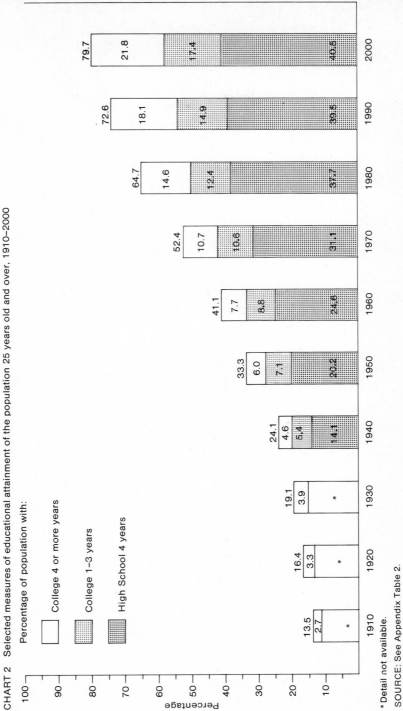

*Detail not available.

SOURCE: See Appendix Table 2.

WHY DO ANYTHING?

CHAPTER

2

This is not a question which was asked in 1636 or in 1870, or even in 1950 or 1960, but it is being asked today. There are, we believe, some strong affirmative answers.

INDIVIDUAL NEEDS AND ASPIRATIONS

Higher education can benefit many more individuals in more ways in the future than it did in the past:

Work More jobs require more training than ever before, and this trend will continue. A college education generally leads to better paying and more satisfying jobs. And jobs tend to be improved in their content, their work environment, and the options associated with them if they are held by persons with a college education. The private returns to a college education, measured by additional net income after taxes as against additional private investment—now runs about 10 percent or more.

Decisions Individuals must make more and more complex decisions, with longer time horizons, as society and its products and services become more complex. A college education leads to greater ability to obtain and analyze facts in the process of making these decisions. College graduates tend to act more effectively in the care of their health, in the purchase of goods and services, in the investment of their money, in the care and education of their children.

Quality of life A college education opens up new interests in the creative arts, in participation in community affairs, in intellectual pursuits.

Life options Going to college generally enhances the ranges of options open to individuals—in jobs, in living locations, in choice of mates, in selection among lifestyles. College education provides both more opportunities for young persons to make choices and a broader basis on which they can evaluate those opportunities and make decisions about them. Chances of finding a satisfactory combination of endeavors and of environments is increased; life becomes potentially more satisfying.

The talents of individuals, in their many dimensions, can be more fully developed by college attendance and need to be more fully developed as the surrounding society grows in scale and complexity.

Higher education can benefit many more individuals in more ways in the future than it did in the past.

SOCIAL REQUIREMENTS AND PROTECTIONS

Society increasingly needs the contributions of higher education.

Society increasingly needs the contributions of higher education:

Skills To find and train talent for the professions and for positions of leadership in political and economic life. The social return on investments in greater skills through education now seems to be of the order of 10 percent or more, with social return narrowly defined as total additional income produced as against all additional investments made.

New and better ideas To conduct the basic and applied research that may create the solutions to the even more complicated and serious problems of the future that now relate to survival itself.

Understanding and tolerance To create greater appreciation of the intricacies of a society in constant change and a sense of being able to cope with these intricacies, and to create a greater spirit of tolerance for the ways and views of other individuals in a national society and an emerging world society marked by great pluralism of beliefs and modes of conduct; and thus to reduce the tendency toward blind reaction to "the ordeal of change" and toward rejection of the unfamiliar in other persons.

World view To broaden the world view of citizens in a world of more intense interactions among cultures, nations, institutions and individuals.

Participation To increase the amount of personal participation of citizens as voters and as contributors to the affairs of the nation, state, and community, and as members of the myriad private groups and organizations of American society, and to increase knowledge by citizens of local, national, and world affairs.

Cultural heritage To help preserve and to add to, and to make more available the creative arts and the scholarship that can so enrich the lives of individuals, and to provide more centers for participation in cultural activities and events. In forwarding the variety and maturity of cultural life, higher education is now a great source of scholarship and of creativity in all areas of cultural development and a major means for the development of greater interest in and more appreciation for the cultural life of the nation.

Social justice To spread greater equality of opportunity to all persons so that they can develop their capacities and their interests; and gradually and partially to reduce inequalities in earned income as more persons are educated out of reliance solely on low-paying jobs and as labor market competition is increased among those persons with greater training.

Ecology To enlarge the understanding of the interconnectedness of the environment and of its fragility over time; to reduce the birthrate as levels of education rise; to expand activities that absorb the attention and energies of people and yet consume few scarce resources and contribute little to pollution—activities that are ecologically sound.

Scholarship To encourage advanced scholarship and the resultant wisdom that may be useful in achieving an understanding of the nature of society and the consequences of individual behavior; to create an environment where dissident ideas contend and the arts of persuasion are perfected so that ideas become tools for a continuing evaluation of society and of the behavior of individuals; to support scholarship that will assist society in its self-renewal and self-advancement.

Experimentation To provide opportunities for trying out alternative lifestyles and modes of thought, some of which may possibly contribute to human welfare generally—though many will not.

Control of power To help train individuals and to devise social means so that the power of the machine, the power of the massive organization, the power of entrenched leadership is less likely to overwhelm man; to help build strength in individuals to confront the more powerful technology and the more powerful social structures of modern society; to help avoid *1984.*

Higher education has made contributions in each of these areas. It is capable of making even more.

Higher education has made contributions in each of these areas.[1] It is capable of making even more. It has made these contributions, of course, with the help of many other types of organizations, and can only make them within a generally supportive social environment; and there are major limitations to what it can do even under the best of circumstances and insurmountable obstacles under the worst of conditions. And higher education has its costs:

[1] See *Technical Notes on the Purposes and Performance of Higher Education,* forthcoming from this Commission, for a further discussion of the benefits of higher education.

In resources—now 2.5 percent of the GNP for current expenditures.

In public tolerance—because the participants in higher education, rightfully, often dissent from the status quo and, wrongfully, in a democracy where democratic alternatives exist, occasionally seek to disrupt it.

In stability—because the rapid changes in industry and society fostered by higher education accentuate the other factors making for rapid and unsettling change in the modern world.

Modern societies are very complex congeries of institutions, with many interchangeable parts. It is conceivable, but barely so, that an industrial society could progress without any system of higher education at all by engaging other institutions to serve the same purposes, but none has ever done so or even tried to do so. Generally, the more progressive the nation, in terms of human liberties and material necessities, the better is its system of higher education. We take this to be a law of social progress.

Generally, the more progressive the nation, in terms of human liberties and material necessities, the better is its system of higher education. We take this to be a law of social progress.

Modern man lives in a world that requires many skills, necessitates many decisions, opens up many options and many possibilities. It is conceivable, but once again barely so, that individuals could gain these skills to the same extent, make these decisions as effectively, and choose among options and possibilities as wisely without access to higher education, but no adequate substitutes have yet been devised.

Education is now changing society, as well as being changed by society, and higher education is more and more potentially capable of exercising leadership within all of education and within society. Higher education, in particular, can help lead to more individual participation in a democratic society, more meaningful work in a more productive economy, and more cultural diversity and creativity in a future world with greater leisure. Thus, whether out of desire or out of necessity, higher education is in a position of prominence in the United States today and is likely to remain so and even become more so in the foreseeable future.

Higher education, in particular, can help lead to more individual participation in a democratic society, more meaningful work in a more productive economy, and more cultural diversity and creativity in a future with greater leisure.

The benefits of higher education, actual and potential, dwarf the costs, whether viewed in monetary or in human terms. Were we to dismantle our system of higher education, or even allow it to deteriorate for very long, the nation would lose immeasurably. And, anything that can be done now or in the future to improve the performance of higher education in the United States will improve also the lives of the many persons who now

Anything that can be done now or in the future to improve the performance of

higher education in the United States will improve also the lives of the many persons who now receive some higher education, the conduct of the many institutions in which all citizens participate, and the welfare of the nation as a whole.

receive some higher education, the conduct of the many institutions in which all citizens participate, and the welfare of the nation as a whole.

Higher education in the United States is a vanguard system among those around the world. How well it develops and in which directions, is, consequently, of more than national importance alone.

PRIORITIES FOR ACTION

SETTING PRIORITIES

CHAPTER

To begin with, there must be a willingness to assess the potentialities of the situation. In our view many constructive programs can be undertaken—every period of crisis, this one included, holds within itself possibilities for forward motion. More doubtful is the existence of a general will to act, to rise above the disappointments of the recent past, but, given the will, there are many possibilities.

Not everything that might be considered good, however, can be done; some good things are impossible—for example, the percentage of the GNP spent on higher education cannot keep on more than doubling as it did in the 1960s, however much this might be desired by some. Of those good things that can be done, not everything can be done at once; resources of money and of attention are limited. Nor are all good things compatible with each other—the more effective use of resources may run against some ways of improving quality. Nor is any single good thing cost-free—every action has a debit account.

The priorities for action that we have chosen are those we believe to be of greatest importance for the foreseeable future, are possible of accomplishment, are reasonably consistent with each other—some even reinforcing each other, and are each well worth their costs. We have been concerned with selecting among all the desirable results that might be wished those that we consider to be attainable and, beyond that, most urgent at this time.

Priorities are different from purposes. Purposes are the overall ends of higher education. Priorities relate to those things that most need to be improved, both as to ends and to means. To some purposes we give a higher current priority than to others, not because they are inherently more important than others, but because more needs to be done and can be done with them at this time than with others. For example, basic research is of the highest importance, but it is more fully advanced at the present time than is the contribution of higher education to equality of opportunity, and so we give the higher priority to equality of opportunity. But in the future, if great progress continues to be made in the direction of greater equality of opportunity and if support of basic research continues to decline, the order might then be reversed.

Where does higher education stand as it assesses its priorities? We believe that it is in a new period of discontinuity, as it was in 1870. Then the issue was the modernization of higher educa-

Many constructive programs can be undertaken —every period of crisis, this one included, holds within itself possibilities of forward motion.

Priorities are different from purposes.

tion—how to adjust to industrial and agricultural expansion, to political populism, to the rise of science. Today the issue is more the humanization of higher education—how to respond to the greater aspirations of more individuals for a higher quality of life, how to adjust to the social facts of more affluence and more leisure, how to incorporate into higher education the rise of the creative arts.

Higher education faces a period of greater diffusion of its activities throughout the population, and greater dispersion geographically—the involvement of more people and places.

Higher education faces a period of greater diffusion of its activities throughout the population, and greater dispersion geographically—the involvement of more people and more places.

This is not to suggest that much, if anything, of what has been done in the past will be taken away, but rather to indicate the central logic of what is being added—which is that higher education, rather than being for some of the people some of the time, is moving more nearly to being available to more nearly all of the people and more nearly all of the time.

Much of what higher education does, such as scholarship and training for the professions, is lasting and is unaffected by the changing nature of the times, and it is of the utmost importance to preserve the purity and the independence of intellect. But each period is defined more by what changes than by what remains the same.

Higher education stands in increasingly closer relations to some of the other segments of the knowledge component of society. It follows, in the lives of individuals, upon primary and secondary education and should be better coordinated with them; it stands beside further education in industry, the military, private specialty schools, and other institutions; it is surrounded by and to some extent participates in other aspects of the knowledge sector of the economy (see Chart 3, page 24). Each of these several segments is important in its own right, but higher education relates more to each and to all of them than does any one other segment; and it is more of the center for new ideas and for standards of intellectual performance than any of the others.

Where higher education stands depends greatly on where American society stands. As we see it, American society is becoming ever more meritocratic in its search for talent; gradually more humane

Where higher education stands depends greatly on where American society stands. As we see it, American society is becoming ever more meritocratic in its search for talent; gradually more egalitarian in the distribution of economic income; gradually more humane in its concern for the health, the education, and the chance for development of all citizens; more

in its concern for the health, the education, and the chance for development of all citizens; more pluralistic in its acceptance of diverse cultures and lifestyles. It will remain, we believe, essentially democratic, its citizens participating actively in setting the general directions for its political, social, and economic institutions.

pluralistic in its acceptance of diverse cultures and lifestyles. It will remain, we believe, essentially democratic, its citizens participating actively in setting the general directions for its political, social, and economic institutions. We see no unresolvable conflicts between a society becoming more meritocratic in selecting talent for business, government, academic, and cultural life and simultaneously becoming more humanitarian in the distribution of income and dignity and chances for a high quality of life. In fact, the perpetuation of a meritocratic society in the area of production may require a more humanitarian society in the area of consumption, and, also, vice versa. Without a more equitable distribution of goods and services and opportunities, the great inequalities of status and power inherent in the meritocratic hierarchy of productive activity may not be politically and socially so viable—and without emphasis upon merit in the productive processes, there will be less available to distribute for consumption. Education is inexorably more and more at the center of a meritocratic society dependent upon many high skills, and of a society seeking to become more humane by aiding the development of each individual human personality.

Some of the priorities we set forth below relate to these new directions, such as more attention to quality; some to the unfinished business of earlier times, such as continued emphasis on equality of opportunity; and some to means, such as more effective governance and use of resources.

Priorities imply action, and a program of action, we believe, is needed. Action in what directions?

Priorities imply action, and a program of action, we believe, is needed. Action in what directions? We suggest:

Clarification of purposes

Preservation and enhancement of quality and diversity

Advancement of social justice

Enhancement of constructive change

Achievement of more effective governance

Assurance of resources and their more effective use.

CHART 3   Expenditures, including forgone income, forgone taxes, and implicit rents, in billions of dollars, estimated roughly for 1970, by major segments of the "knowledge" sector of American society

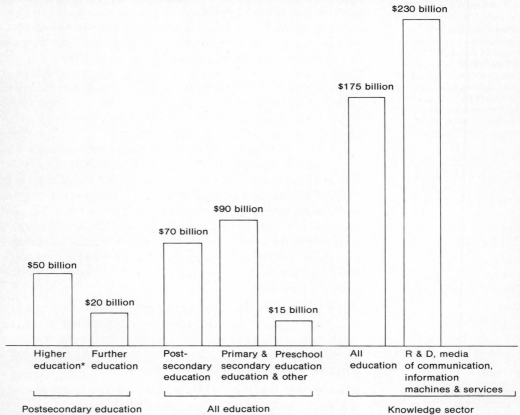

*Includes all of higher education, including non-degree-credit studies.

SOURCE: Estimated by the Carnegie Commission staff using the "knowledge industry" structure proposed by Machlup (1962). Components, other than formal education, such as research and development, media of communication, information machines, and information services, have been assumed to grow at the same rate as formal education and research and development during the period 1958 to 1970.

CLARIFICA-
TION
OF
PURPOSES

CHAPTER

Lionel Trilling has commented upon "the growing intellectual recessiveness of college and university faculties, their reluctance to formulate any coherent theory for higher education, to discover what its best purposes are . . ." (Trilling, 1972, p. 29). But not only faculties alone, presidents and trustees also often seem to share this reluctance.

The public has a right to be concerned. Higher education, as it faces the public, has appeared to be changing some of its purposes, to some degree at least, in unwise directions. Disruption for a time went far beyond the historic limits of dissent, and disruption has had its faculty as well as its student supporters. Some faculties in recent years began taking institutionalized positions on political issues of an off-campus nature and abandoned the traditional position of political neutrality by the institution as such. Campuses took less responsibility for the individual conduct of their students and, simultaneously, often showed too little conception of or interest in the nature of a constructive environment for student development. "General education" began to decay on many campuses and nothing was put in its place. Standards of teaching were often sacrificed to other activities. The colleges seemed intent upon processing more and more graduates almost without regard to the general or specific needs of society, as in the case of the surplus of Ph.D.'s, albeit that they had inadequate forecasting data with which to work. Higher education, on occasion, even seemed to have lost faith in the mind, and there were those within it who followed the "ideological trend which rejects and seeks to discredit the very concept of the mind" (ibid., p. 30). Thus, certain historic positions have been temporarily or permanently abandoned—sometimes wisely, sometimes not—by some segments of higher education, but seemingly always without full deliberation and certainly without adequate explanation to interested publics of the reasons for the changes.

Higher education has appeared to be changing some of its purposes, to some degree at least, in unwise directions.

Academics, as well as the public, have a right—even a duty— to be concerned about changing purposes, and the methods used in carrying them out. For the sake of their own intellectual integrity as well as for the sake of public understanding and support, they should also be concerned about the use of disruption, about institutional participation in the political arena, about the quality of the total environment provided for students, about the nature of an effective general education in the modern world, about the level of academic standards, about the

Academics, as well as the public, have a right—even a duty—to be concerned about changing purposes, and the methods used in carrying them out.

efficient transmission of the most useful skills, about the place of the mind in the hierarchy of human capacities.

We have set forth in one of our reports what we believe to be the major purposes for the total system of higher education in the period ahead:

Advancing the intellectual and professional capacity of individual students within a constructive campus environment

Enhancing human capability in society at large through training, research, and service

Increasing social justice through greater equality of opportunity to obtain an advanced education

Advancing learning for its own sake through science, scholarship, and the creative arts; and for the sake of public interest and consumption

Evaluating society, for the benefit of its self-renewal, through individual scholarship and persuasion

Higher education needs to clarify what it thinks it is about and place this clarified set of purposes before the nation.

Whether this series of purposes is an adequate one or not— and we believe that it is—higher education needs to clarify what it thinks it is about and to place this clarified set of purposes before the nation; so also should each campus, for its own constituencies, realizing that the purposes of most campuses will be more selective than those for higher education in its entirety.

There should be some new aspirations, some new visions.

Higher education had a dominant set of purposes when it was first established in the United States in 1636 and for a long time thereafter, and it drew selective but devoted support for them. A revised and even largely new set of purposes was developed after the Civil War, and it, in turn, drew sustained and much broader support. Once again, higher education needs to reaffirm its sense of purpose, for its own sake and for the sake of public understanding and assent. Higher education needs clearer answers to the question of "why?" A restoration of a sense of confidence and of clear forward motion depends upon the success of such an undertaking. There has been no basic discussion of purposes, engaged in widely within higher education, for a century. There should be some new aspirations, some new visions.

PRESERVATION AND ENHANCEMENT OF QUALITY AND DIVERSITY

CHAPTER

Higher education after World War II went through a period when the emphasis was upon quantity, upon vast expansion of what was already being done. The period ahead, of necessity, will see less emphasis on quantitative growth. Attention can now turn and should turn more to the quality of the effort.

This is not to suggest that quality suffered during the two and one-half decades of rapid increases in enrollments and research activity; in fact, quality was generally maintained, with the possible exception of some of the many new Ph.D. programs in institutions not well staffed or equipped to provide them. Thus the problem is not one of restoration of quality, but of its preservation and improvement; and quality, of course, is of highest importance to the academic endeavor.

One of the interesting—and, to some, surprising—discoveries of recent times has been that quality and quantity are not necessarily inconsistent with each other in the academic world, and even that, in some situations, quantity can make it possible to add to quality. The public university, for example, often has had a better chance to add on and to finance academic segments of high quality within the context of great size; out of its total resources, a margin for excellence has been made available. On the international level, mass enrollments may hold down the average performance of all school students on standardized tests but, by finding talent throughout society, the performance of the most select groups of students in mass enrollment nations tends to be at about the same level as those of select groups in non-mass enrollment nations or may even be elevated somewhat above them.[1] The academic performance of the total age group, if it were subject to testing, would, of course, also be expected to rise since larger proportions are students and smaller proportions are nonstudents, and nonstudents presumably would test out at lower levels of achievement. "More" has not always, or even usually, meant "worse," as so many British scholars, in particular, once thought was inevitable.

Quality, however, should now be of growing importance; hence many of our reports have been concerned with qualitative improvements.

[1] Comber and Keeves (1973) and Hechinger (1973). The studies involved show that schools do make a difference more generally, particularly in science and mathematics and at the higher levels of instruction farther removed from family and neighborhood influences.

RESEARCH

Federal support for scientific research should be maintained at the same level as in the 1960s, and on a steady basis in relation to the GNP. More priority should be given to basic research, with more funds for the social sciences and humanities, with awards to individual projects on the basis of merit as determined by panels of academic experts, and with flexibility in assignments of funds to reflect changing possibilities from one field to another.

TEACHING

There should be equal reward for teaching as for research, except for research at the highest levels of competence. Students should be involved in the evaluation of teaching. "Codes of Teaching Responsibility" should be adopted to guide faculty members in their conduct and to inform students of what they can expect. There should be greater use of the new electronic technology as a supplement to and an alternative for traditional teaching. Libraries should be converted into "learning centers." More provision should be made for independent study by students and for credit by examination. The use of the doctor of arts degree with emphases on a broader subject matter training and on supervised teaching experience should be extended as an alternative to the Ph.D. for faculty members who will be engaged primarily in teaching—and teacher training should be generally improved.

CURRICULUM REFORM

Renovation of general education should be achieved by providing optional programs directed toward "broad learning experiences," as we have sought to set them forth. Greater attention should be paid to the creative arts and to world cultures. Earlier contact is needed with actual professional problems in such fields as medicine and law. More care is needed in avoiding duplication of work already taken in high school—an overlap of two-thirds of a year's work now often occurs; there should also be more attention by colleges to the design of admission policies to allow greater curricular freedom at the high school level. There should be more participation by students in curricular development and review. The same level of support should be provided for lower- as for upper-division students; the cost ratio now averages about 1 to 1.5. In large institutions, deans of undergraduate instruction should be appointed to raise the standards, as was done historically by deans of graduate divisions. More encouragement of independent study is desirable.

CONSTRUCTIVE CAMPUS ENVIRONMENT

More use of "cluster colleges" and other methods of structuring students and faculty members into face-to-face groupings is needed. There should be more mixing of persons from different age groups, both in classes and in out-of-class contacts. More opportunities should be provided for students to engage in work and service experiences. More attention should be given to advising—on personal, academic, and vocational matters. Each of these would add to our conception of a more constructive environment on campus.

SERVICE

There should now be more faculty consultation on urban, as earlier there was on rural, problems. More assistance should be given by health science centers to local health care institutions, and to the creation of area health education centers— first recommended by the Commission in 1970 and provided for in federal legislation in 1971. Across the nation, there should be a wider spread of community colleges—with their cultural and adult education programs—so that 95 percent of all persons will be within commuting distance of a college. More programs that pay special attention to students drawn from minority groups, and that are available to part-time and to recurrent students returning to college later in life, should be created.

PRESERVATION OF UNIQUE INSTITUTIONS

Colleges originally founded for Negroes and private liberal arts colleges are particularly to be preserved. The former are a special "national asset"—as we have described them; the latter have provided to all of higher education elements of diversity of approach, models of attention to individual students, opportunities to put innovations into practice relatively easily, and standards for institutional independence. We have proposed special financial assistance to these colleges, and a narrowing of the tuition gap with public institutions.

"Elite" institutions of all types—colleges and universities— should be protected and encouraged as a source of scholarship and leadership training at the highest levels. They should not be homogenized in the name of egalitarianism. Such institutions, whether public or private, should be given special support for instruction and research, and for the ablest of graduate students; they should be protected by policies on differentiation of functions. "All civilized countries . . . depend upon a thin clear stream of excellence to provide new ideas, new techniques, and the statesmanlike treatment of complex social and political problems" (Ashby, 1971, p. 101).

EFFECTIVE SIZE

We have been concerned that some campuses are too small to have a well-rounded academic program for their students, and that others are too large to have a sense of cohesion and an effective governance, particularly at the departmental level, with faculty and student concerns too fractionated. We have suggested "peril points" below which and above which campuses should be concerned as to whether their quality of effort may be impeded by either too small or too large a scale.

	MINIMUM FTE ENROLLMENT	MAXIMUM FTE ENROLLMENT
DOCTORAL-GRANTING INSTITUTIONS	5,000	20,000
COMPREHENSIVE COLLEGES	5,000	10,000
LIBERAL ARTS COLLEGES	1,000	2,500
COMMUNITY COLLEGES	2,000	5,000

MAINTENANCE OF ACADEMIC STANDARDS

Some professors in some institutions have greatly reduced their expectations of students, have abandoned all differential grading, have renounced any standards in the name of meeting the standards of the individual student. We greatly regret this. There should be no erosion of intellectual standards.

Most of these suggested means of improving quality depend more upon better policies than they do on more money. Taken together, their adoption could substantially elevate the quality of the performance of higher education.

Most of these suggested means of improving quality depend more upon better policies than they do on more money. Taken together, their adoption could substantially elevate the quality of the performance of higher education. But money is important. We have suggested that support should rise per student per year at about the historic rate of the general level of inflation plus 2.5 percent. It is now less than this for many institutions.

Higher quality in teaching, in curricular offerings, in campus environments, in research and service; and greater diversity among and within, and greater effectiveness of, institutions are clearly possible and highly desirable. The "tidal wave" of students of the 1960s was handled with great success; the new imperative is a more modest wave of interest in quality, in intensive rather than extensive growth—albeit that the former is more difficult than the latter to achieve and can never be doubled, as were enrollments, in the course of a single decade.

The "tidal wave" of students of the 1960s was handled with great success; the new imperative is a more modest wave of interest in quality, in intensive rather than extensive growth.

ADVANCE-
MENT OF
SOCIAL
JUSTICE

CHAPTER

6

The United States of America began with the high aspiration that in this then new nation each person should have an equal opportunity to participate as a voter in the political process and to develop his talents and interests to the best of his ability and in keeping with the degree of his personal desire; that no artificial or unreasonable barriers should stand between the individual citizen and his potential contributions to the political process, to economic endeavor, and to personal self-advance-ment; that society should aid the individual affirmatively to realize his capacities as a citizen, as a productive worker, and as an individual seeking a high quality of life. This high aspira-tion has never been realized. Slavery was once the greatest barrier to its fulfillment, but continuing discrimination against members of regional, ethnic, and racial groups and lack of adequate opportunities for still others has also long stood in its way. We are now approaching 1976 with the great dream of 1776 still awaiting fulfillment—not perfect fulfillment, for that probably lies outside the capacity of imperfect man, but fulfill-ment in terms of certain basic fundamentals.

THE PROMISE OF EDUCATION

Education, from the beginning, was thought by some to have a major role to play in the attainment of this special aspiration for greater human welfare. There was the belief that a basic education should be the right of all persons, and that those with greater abilities should have the chance to advance to such levels as their talents might warrant. Thomas Jefferson, for example, urged a "crusade against ignorance" to "establish and improve the law for educating the common people."[1] He also believed that "there is a natural aristocracy among men. The grounds of this are virtue and talents,"[2] and urged addi-tional education, at public expense, for those demonstrating special ability at the lower levels of schooling. "The object is to bring into action that mass of talents which lies buried in poverty in every country."[3]

The United States of America began with the high aspiration that in this then new nation each per-son should have an equal opportunity to participate as a voter in the political process, and to develop talents and interests to the best of his ability and in keeping with the degree of his personal desire.

This high aspiration has never been realized.

[1] Letter from Thomas Jefferson to George Wythe, written from Paris, August 13, 1786 (Lee, 1961, p. 100).

[2] Letter from Thomas Jefferson to John Adams, October 28, 1813 (ibid., p. 162).

[3] Letter from Thomas Jefferson to M. Correa, November 25, 1817 (Honeywell, 1931, p. 148).

The initial emphasis was on the creation of a universally avail-able system of primary education, then of secondary education, and now of higher education—open to all as each is qualified by age and ability. All three systems have, of course, existed throughout history, but they have moved in successive waves from selective-choice to mass-access to universal-access status; from service to the few, to the many, to potentially all.

These advancements, step by step, to a condition of universality of access, from the primary to the secondary to the tertiary level, have reflected both the increasing capacity of society to afford each advance and the rising need for it to take place. Society has had the augmenting wealth to build more schools, to forgo the labor of those in school, and to prepare and sup-port teachers. Society and the individuals within it have desired higher levels of education as jobs have become more skilled, as citizenship has required a larger amount of more complex information, and as the process of life has involved the making of more and more decisions in connection with the enlarging range of options open to individuals as consumers.

Education, and particu-larly higher education, has been given an in-creasing responsibility for the realization of equal-ity of opportunity.

Education, and particularly higher education, has been given an increasing responsibility for the realization of equality of opportunity, particularly as the level of job requirements has risen. But this responsibility is borne by many other segments of society as well: child health care must be adequate, jobs must be open on the basis of ability without discrimination, and neighborhood living locations must be available without discrimination. Realization of equality of opportunity is a com-plex process that involves many institutions and many policies, including the institutions and the policies of higher education.

Higher education in 1870 enrolled 2 percent of the college-age group; in 1970, it enrolled nearly 50 percent. Access has spread from higher- to lower-income levels, and from members of the majority to members of minority groups. Progress has been particularly rapid over the past decade. In the fall of 1972, blacks were represented among new enrollees in college in almost the same proportions as they were represented among high school graduates.[4] The proportion 10 years ago was more nearly 2 to 3 than 1 to 1.

[1] Just under 50 percent of both blacks and whites who had just graduated from high school enrolled in college (Young, 1973).

Yet there is still a substantial distance to go. Blacks do not graduate from high school in the same proportions as whites, and their proportions at the graduate level of higher education are also low. Spanish-origin Americans, including Puerto Ricans and Chicanos, and American Indians are underrepresented at all levels of higher education, in a ratio of about 1 or less to 2 for the rest of the relevant population. Appendix Table 3 sets forth the comparative representation of students by income levels of their families, by measured academic ability, and by sex for the years 1957, 1961, and 1967, and it shows, among other things, but of special importance, that young persons with the higher levels of ability, particularly women, have not had equal chances of attendance when they come from lower-income families. The rate of improvement in attendance for high-ability young persons from the lower socioeconomic quartiles, however, has been impressive.

THE CONTRIBUTIONS OF HIGHER EDUCATION

All remnants of inequality of educational opportunity due to race, sex, family level of income, and geographical location should be overcome substantially by 1980 and as completely as possible by the year 2000.

We have been concerned, in a number of our reports, with how higher education might make a greater contribution to the realization of equality of opportunity. We believe that major steps can be taken now, and that all remnants of inequality of educational opportunity due to race, sex, family level of income, and geographical location should be overcome substantially by 1980 and as completely as possible by the year 2000.[5] We view such a potential contribution by higher education to be of enormous potential benefit to American democracy. We suggest in particular:

(1) The creation of a sufficiency of *open-access places,* particularly at the lower-division level, defined as places available at low or no net tuition and within commuting distance for all high school graduates who wish to attend. We have recommended the spread of community colleges in all populous areas throughout the United States. We have been particularly concerned with the availability of open-access places in metropolitan areas. We have set forth, state by state and metropolitan

[5] We recognize that some sources of inequality of educational opportunity, such as those based on mental capacity and on family efforts at education in the home, are not subject to elimination and that efforts to eliminate them would involve heavy costs.

area by metropolitan area, the deficits that we believe to exist (see Appendix Tables 4 and 5); but it should be noted that a number of these deficits have already been overcome since we issued our listings. We note that many state plans now make reference to our findings.

(2)   The improvement of old and the creation of new *alternative channels to life and work,* in addition to college attendance. We have favored universal access to higher education but not universal attendance. Many young persons do not want to go to college, including some who are already there—we have estimated these "reluctant attenders" as amounting to at least 5 percent and perhaps as high as 12 percent of the college population in recent years. And many jobs do not require college attendance. Consequently we support the enhancement of other channels: including on-the-job training, proprietary schools, apprenticeship programs, education in the military, education by off-campus extension work, and national service opportunities. Concern should spread to educational opportunities for the total age group and not for college attenders alone.

(3)   The *financing of student costs* where there is inability to meet them from personal resources. We believe that such inability now exists, in quite varying degrees, for students coming from families in the lower half of the income range and perhaps somewhat above this level. We have supported improved programs of grants, work-study, and loans. The Higher Education Act of 1972 (technically the "Amendments of 1972"), with its Basic Opportunity Grants, is a great step forward. Both Congress and the President drew on our earlier proposal of a "Civilian GI Bill of Rights" in developing this legislation. This program now needs to be both fully funded and in some ways improved. The State Incentive Grants program, included in the same legislation, should be funded as soon as possible in order to encourage the states to supplement the federal program. Work-study support should be continued and expanded to include the larger numbers of students as they enroll. The federal loan system needs major and fundamental improvements. We have suggested the creation of a National Student Loan Bank. The United States is, however, despite these needed improvements, getting much closer to having an adequate and well-balanced student support program than

ever before. But there is need to move beyond this to future consideration of a program of "two-years-in-the-bank," as we once called it, or an "educational endowment," for all persons who seek postcompulsory education to improve their paths into and within life and work, whether by way of college or through other educational channels.

(4) The *adjustment* of the postsecondary system of education *to students from a wider variety of backgrounds.* Admissions policies have been and should be reviewed. We have suggested special admissions provisions for disadvantaged students where their ability and the special assistance of the college will make possible their meeting, in full, the academic standards of the college within a reasonable period of time, and certainly by graduation. Remedial work may be necessary. Colleges should also make provision for the cultural interests of more of the members of their increasingly varied student populations.

(5) The *recruitment into faculty and administrative positions of more women and more members of minority groups.* Women are now in such positions to about one-half or more of reasonable expectations, and members of minority groups to about one-third. Their greater presence would contribute not only to enhanced social justice but also to the effectiveness of higher education by providing models for women and minority students to emulate, a reservoir of greater sensitivity to their special interests and problems—more "mentors," and generally more sources of talent than are now available. We have suggested that special efforts be made to recruit such persons into the "pool" for consideration when appointments are made, and that their special potential contributions be weighed as a factor in considering the overall excellence of a department, school, or college.

Just as we strongly favor greater equality of opportunity through higher education, we oppose with the same vigor the now increasingly popular doctrine of equality of academic rewards.

Just as we strongly favor greater equality of opportunity through higher education, we oppose with the same vigor the now increasingly popular doctrine of equality of academic rewards —as through abolition of all grades in all universities, granting of degrees on a time-served basis or even on the basis of time not served, and promotions of faculty members on the basis of seniority alone. We believe that adherence to such a doctrine would lead to a gross degradation of academic standards. We also believe that it would be unfair to give students and faculty members with greater ability and who show greater effort equalized rewards regardless of their ability and their effort, and that such a doctrine would be unfair to society more generally by denying it full access to contributions "from each according to his ability" as made possible by identifying special talent and helping to develop it for its maximum usefulness. For the sake of the welfare of the academic enterprise, of the justice of differential treatment for those who perform differentially, and of the social advancement of society through enhanced human capability, we categorically oppose this doctrine of equalization of academic rewards.

The unfinished business of 1776 must soon be completed. The goal of equality of opportunity is a superior one, and long promised. The United States long ago undertook a great experiment in pursuit of a high goal—an experiment in the use of education to obtain greater equality of opportunity for all its citizens. It has led and continues to lead the world in the pursuit of this experiment. How well it does is watched around the world, and most of all by those of its own citizens who have not yet enjoyed adequate equality of opportunity.

COUNTERATTACKS

Attacks, from at least two directions, are made on this emphasis on equality of opportunity. We shall take them up in order.

The supporters of the first attack say that the true goal is equality of income, not equality of opportunity, which is only an "equal chance to become unequal" (Halsey, 1973); and that education, including higher education, makes little, if any, contribution to equality of income. To begin with, the factual finding is wrong. Education in underdeveloped societies often adds to inequality by raising some persons to comparatively very high income levels. In developed societies, including the United States, it seems to contribute gradually and modestly to equalization of earned incomes as the more highly educated come to be in more plentiful supply. Using the figures of Jencks (in *Inequality*), Coleman shows a remarkable correspondence between more equality of education and more equality in income for the period 1929 to 1970.[6]

Additionally, a contribution to equality of income is not the one and only basic test of the effectiveness of education; it is only a subsidiary test. More basic tests are:

■ Contributions to equality of opportunity, to the creation of a more open society, to elimination of an inherited class structure, to giving individuals a better chance to express their talents and interests and to be rewarded for special competence and effort and personal achievement. Education, including higher education, is the main instrument of equality of opportunity in an industrial society requiring a high level of employment skills from many of its citizens.

■ Contributions to the general level of economic productivity, to advanced skills, to better judgment, to drawing forth talent and effort—and thus to more goods and better services. The contributions here are clearly of a high order.

■ Contributions to noneconomic aspects of individual lives, such as ability to make decisions; and to the noneconomic performance of society, as in greater participation in political processes. These contributions also are substantial.

Neither a "closed" class society nor a flat-out equalized one, in terms of rewards, would provide the same chance for individuals to advance themselves in accordance with their abilities and interests, or would draw forth the same degree of talent to be applied to the tasks of society.

Neither a "closed" class society nor a flat-out equalized one, in terms of rewards, would provide the same chance for individuals to advance themselves in accordance with their abilities and interests, or would draw forth the same degree of talent to be applied to the tasks of society.

The supporters of the second line of attack argue that greater equality of opportunity will necessarily reduce standards. There

[6] See James S. Coleman, "Equality of Opportunity and Equality of Results," *Harvard Educational Review*, February 1973. He shows the following "comparison of changes in the variation of income and education for selected years, 1929 to 1970" where 1929 is taken as the base year and lower figures show greater equality:

YEAR	INCOME	EDUCATION
1929	1.0	1.0
1935–36	0.88	0.89
1946	0.71	0.71
1960	0.67	0.67
1968	0.59	0.60
1970	0.61	0.55

is no reason in theory to expect this, for greater equality of opportunity should add to the spirit of competition and to the wealth of top talent found and developed. In fact, in the United States the academic quality of students in higher education does not appear thus far to have been reduced by the movement to mass higher education and may have been raised somewhat (Taubman & Wales, 1972). A policy or practice of universal attendance in college, as compared with equality of opportunity through universal access to college, might very well, however, reduce standards.

Thus we consider the achievement of greater equality of opportunity to be a major purpose of higher education in the United States. Those who seek the single goal of equality of incomes will understandably find means other than education more appealing and will consider that education does too little and does it too late for their purposes. Those who raise the banner of standards against equality of opportunity may find that standards can better be raised by other methods than by return to a more closed, more hereditary society.

ALTERNATIVE APPROACHES

To achieve greater equality of opportunity through higher education, within the range of possible policies between (a) the continuation of class and racial and sexual barriers on the one hand and (b) enforced equal outcomes to each individual on the other, choice may be made among six general positions:

(1)   Removal of discriminatory barriers against entrance

(2)   Equalization of opportunity and consideration at all levels and in all ways

(3)   Special consideration, because of past inequalities, in admissions policies, in search efforts for talent, in remedial assistance, and in financial aids in order to provide a fair chance for each person, but with the expectation that individual academic results will depend on talent and effort

(4)   Quotas group by group—the doctrine of proportional representation at all levels, in all fields, at all campuses

(5)   Lottery—equal individual chances for a "winning ticket"

(6)   Compensatory efforts to redress in large part or in full all prior disabilities by whatever it takes to make possible equal academic outcomes in terms of competence.

Our position is generally (3) above. We believe that it is better for individuals and for society to approximate reasonable proportions among broad groups through achievement and over a period of time, than it is to seek immediate and exact proportions through assignment.

Higher education historically has had some negative impacts on equality of opportunity for many women and for many members of minority groups. It should now move over to the positive side.

Higher education historically has had some negative impacts on equality of opportunity for many women and for many members of minority groups. It should now move over to the positive side. Educational justice is a great engine of change, helping to lead to social justice more generally, and, through greater justice, to greater liberty for all and to more fraternity.

We start where we are. We assume an equal pool of intellectual ability among men and women, among members of majority and minority groups. We expect that higher education, in the foreseeable future, will help to draw persons of high ability in about equal proportions from all groups, and that before long the professions and the occupations that recruit from higher education will generally have persons from all groups in about equal proportions to their individual abilities as demonstrated in fair competition. Higher education can still do much more where it has done much already. The voices of despair should be rejected.

The United States is now meeting a new series of problems as it moves along the path of greater equality of opportunity through higher education—such as creation of black studies programs, introduction of remedial work, recruitment into faculties of more women and members of minority groups. But these problems are the problems of progress, not of retrogression or of stagnation; substantial further progress is possible in the future.

What began with such great expectations so long ago can lead in the foreseeable future to a substantial triumph of the good will of men toward men through greater equality of opportunity achieved through higher education and through other improved educational channels to life and to work.

What began with such great expectations so long ago can lead in the foreseeable future to a substantial triumph of the good will of men toward men through greater equality of opportunity achieved through higher education and through other improved educational channels to life and to work.

Our first report was entitled *Quality and Equality.* These continue to be among our highest priorities, and we consider them compatible with each other as goals.

ENHANCE-MENT OF CONSTRUCTIVE CHANGE

CHAPTER 7

Higher education of its own accord usually changes its structures and policies slowly. Aside from the normal tendencies of all established institutions, there are at least three special reasons for reluctance to change: (1) higher education by its very nature is oriented, in substantial part, to preservation of past records, to the teaching of history, to perpetuation of traditions—it has a strong and necessary historical predisposition; (2) faculty members are central to its governance and, like many other professional groups, they rely heavily on very substantial collegial consent before making changes and on the judgment especially of their older and more academically prestigious members, and there is a tradition of not raising controversial problems unless absolutely necessary; and (3) a continuity of academic mores—including the tenets of academic freedom, the preservation of high standards of scholarship, and the cherishing of a sense of stability of structure—is important to the effective conduct of academic work, to the sense that the environment is secure and that individual activity can proceed confidently within it.

But change does come, and more of it more steadily in the American system than in most others. Change came quite gradually until the Civil War—including some relaxation of *in loco parentis* policies and some addition of "modern" subjects to the curriculum. It advanced with great rapidity from 1870 to 1910 with the introduction of science, of a new emphasis upon graduate study, of the idea of service to society, of elective subjects for students. It has proceeded since then at an unsteady pace but generally more slowly, with the rise of the community colleges, the transformation of normal schools and teachers colleges into comprehensive colleges, the extension of research activity into new institutions and new fields, the development of new international concerns, the acceptance of policies of universal access, the adaptation to the interests of minority-group students, among other developments.[1] At all times the changes that come most easily and most constantly are in sub-

Higher education of its own accord usually changes its structures and policies slowly.

But change does come, and more of it more steadily in the American system than in most others.

[1] The list of new developments undertaken by colleges and universities in the past decade is particularly impressive. It includes: revised admission requirements to bring in more members of minority groups, deferred admissions, stopouts, substantial reduction of *in loco parentis* rules, introduction of "black studies" and similar programs, more counseling facilities, more attention to the creative arts, more independent study, greater use of pass-fail grading in courses outside the concentration major, introduction of remedial work, and placement of students on committees, among others.

ject-matter content, as new discoveries are made and old ideas are revised, through the actions of individual faculty members; the "map of learning" as drawn by scholarship undergoes incessant revisions. Changes in structures and policies that require group decision making usually proceed far more slowly.

FORCES FOR AND AGAINST CHANGE

Change, once again, as from 1870 to 1910, now seems likely to proceed at an accelerated rate.

Change, once again, as from 1870 to 1910, now seems likely to proceed at an accelerated rate—not so fundamental in its essence as in that earlier period, but still substantial. The period 1970 to 2000 may prove to be the second most active period of change in the history of American higher education:

■ There are *new types of students,* more of them drawn from among minorities and low-income families but more of them also coming from the more affluent classes—many in the former group are more vocationally oriented and some in the latter group are more inclined toward political activity than have been most students in earlier times.

■ There are *new interests among students,* regardless of their origin, as in service activity, in creative expression, in their "emotional growth," in social problems.

■ There is more and more *new knowledge* to be introduced into each field and into the content of general education—often more than can be absorbed easily.

■ There is a *new job market,* less capable of readily absorbing all college graduates, more fluctuating in its specific demands for trained talent.

■ There are *new social problems* as a basis for research and service, such as the problems of the metropolis and the physical environment.

■ There is *new technology* available, the most important for higher education in 500 years.

These new developments will press for changes in a context where other, and contrary, forces will also be at work. Against change will be:

■ The *rising age level of faculty members* (the median age will rise by about one-half a year each year from 1970 to 1990) as fewer new hires are made and older persons are protected by tenure and seniority practices.

■ The *decline in enrollment growth* and in the amount of new funds—change will need to come more as a replacement than as an add-on, and this is a difficult way to make change.

■ The advent of *collective bargaining* with its emphasis upon formal rules and policies, and its purpose of protecting established faculty interests.

■ The current *survivalist mentality* of higher education, particularly among administrators but among many faculty members as well—to hang on to as much of the past as possible, to avoid trouble, to follow the political adage of the Third Republic in France that you can survive in public office provided you do nothing. The attitude is often one of maximum gain at *no* cost— the "maximin" principle; and since all institutional gains of importance have costs, the no-cost doctrine means no gains of importance. This is not only the result of the instinct of faculty members and administrators who feel themselves (often correctly) as being on the defensive, but also of the actions of many boards of trustees in selecting "consensual" administrators (concerned solely with mere consent) during and after a period of campus disruption rather than the "builders" who were selected for the earlier period of enormous campus expansion. The rational approach for a consensual administrator, who wants to hold on to his job, is to take no risks, to assume a posture of low visibility, to say nothing but to say it well— while still being "with it." He does often face a delicate balance of forces, many negative veto groups, and a situation where little can be done that will not upset somebody. The graceful protection of the status quo is the course of action for survival. On the other hand, however, administrators—if they want to act —are now less immobilized by attention to controversies than they were in recent years.

Ranged in favor of change will be:

■ *Student activism,* albeit at much lower levels than during the second half of the 1960s but still above historical levels both on-campus and in lobbying activities off-campus.

■ *Greater student choice* among campuses as student-aid provisions, both federal and state, give students wider selection among campuses, and as students, in any event, become more mobile socially and geographically.

■ The greater *scramble for students* as enrollment increases decline and then turn into decreases, as the sellers' market turns into a buyers' market and as the buyers have greater latitude in their choices.

■ *Greater public input,* through governors, legislative committees and coordinating councils, into higher education, as external institutions have more to say about how higher education conducts itself.

The most universally intense pressure for change may well turn out to be the shortage of students.

The most universally intense pressure for change may well turn out to be the shortage of students, as compared with places available for them, particularly in the 1980s. This will lead to efforts by many colleges to enlarge their pool of potential students by accepting more adults and more part-time enrollees regardless of age and to the acceptance of more community college transfers by four-year colleges; to greater endeavors at competitive recruitment; and to attempts to make each campus more attractive by holding down tuition and by improving programs from a student point of view.

On balance, we expect that the need for changes and the superiority of the forces pressing for change—particularly the greater competition for students, will lead to a period of accelerated change, subject to constant challenge by adherents of the status quo. Higher education in the United States has shown its capacity to change in the past and is under pressures to change in the present and on into the foreseeable future.

In general, we have favored reform in three directions: toward more options for students in their attendance patterns; toward more diversity of programs both as among and within individual institutions, thus expanding the range of choice for students; and toward enrichment of programs.

What forms might constructive change take? We have been concerned with this question in several of our reports. In general, we have favored reform in three directions: toward more options for students in their attendance patterns; toward more diversity of programs both as among and within individual institutions, thus expanding the range of choice for students; and toward enrichment of programs.

Students vary greatly in their capacities and in the intensity of their interests. They are generally capable—or at least as capable as anyone else—in many situations of making decisions among alternatives that directly affect themselves. They will be more satisfied with their situations if they are able, within reasonable limits, to structure—student by student—a combination of alternatives that each student believes will best fit his or her individual wishes.

OPTIONS

We have suggested these options among others:

- To go to college or not to go, with less pressure from parents and the labor market, and more alternative channels to select among.
- To be admitted to, but to defer entrance into college.
- To "stop-out" while in college for the sake of work or service experience or travel. Our Commission coined this word, which has now become popular, to convey a constructive aspect to the earlier denigrating term of drop-out.
- To operate within a two-year planning module with a degree available every two years. Thus we have proposed greater use of the associate in arts degree, including its use within four-year colleges, and introduction of a two-year graduate degree, the master of philosophy.
- To have variable time options for getting a degree. We have, in particular, supported the idea of a three-year option for the B.A. degree in order to reduce the duplication of work between high school and college, to allow time for stop-outs, to permit earlier entrance into graduate programs, and generally to save the time of students. But a five-year option, as well as others, should also be made available. Several colleges and universities, relying in part on our recommendations, are now introducing such variable time options.
- To choose between the doctor of arts degree, more oriented toward teaching and broad subject matter, and the Ph.D.
- To attend college more easily on a part-time basis and as older adults.
- To take nontraditional programs, such as those offered by the Open University in Britain—although quite traditional, in this instance, in content. We have initiated the idea of Learning Pavilions where students of any age can stop in to study and to discuss their studies.

We recognize that some of these options reduce the chances of a common culture among college graduates within which people communicate, but this has been happening anyway and we believe the gains will outweigh the losses.

DIVERSITY

American higher education has been marked by comparatively great diversity among institutions, reflecting the pluralism of American culture. This diversity has been reduced as what were once single sex colleges have gone coeducational, as formerly special purpose colleges have taken on more comprehensive programs, as originally regional and religiously oriented colleges have lost their local and sectarian characters. Some of this has been all to the good, but the general overall tendency has been toward homogenization.

Some of the best of the old diversity should be consciously maintained and some new forms of diversity created.

Some of the best of the old diversity should be consciously maintained and some new forms of diversity created. We have supported in particular:

■ Deliberate preservation of "effective" diversity where it now exists among campuses, and creation of new campuses or segments of campuses with built-in elements of uniqueness. Coordinating councils, in particular, should sponsor differentiation of functions among segments of higher education, subject-matter specialization among individual campuses, and a variety of styles of performance; so also should multicampus systems.

■ Creation of cluster colleges within larger institutions, each with its own character; and encouragement of separate identities among professional schools.

■ Preservation of such unique institutions as the colleges founded for Negroes.

■ Development of a series of broad learning experiences, as we have recommended in our report on *Reform on Campus,* from among which students might choose for their general education, rather than the more rigid programs of the past based on set, and often quite artificial, requirements; or rather than no program at all as is increasingly and even more disastrously the case. The goal should be a broad education in addition to competency in one or more subject-matter areas.

Such structural diversity, of course, adds to the options available to students—the granting of student aid on a "free choice of institution" basis, as we have supported, makes such options more widely open to choice.

ENRICHMENT

Higher education can be enriched in many ways, and often by better policy rather than by more money. Our suggestions have included:

- More inspired teaching and more effective courses of study
- More attention to the creative arts and to the study of world cultures
- More availability of service and work opportunities
- More mixing of age groups on campus
- More development of the library as a learning center, more use of electronic technology as an alternative to traditional methods of instruction, and more opportunities for individualized instruction
- More use of advising and counseling services relating to academic choices, job opportunities, and personal adjustments
- More concern for a constructive campus environment for the developmental growth of students

We recognize, in particular, the great difficulties in providing effective advising and counseling services, and in defining a "constructive" environment.

These several suggestions for more options, more diversity, and greater enrichment of programs would in totality, if effectuated, lead to a substantial amount of constructive change—even to a minor revolution of free choice, of individualization of higher education.

These several suggestions for more options, more diversity, and greater enrichment of programs would in totality, if effectuated, lead to a substantial amount of constructive change— even to a minor revolution, a revolution of free choice, of individualization of higher education, and would go quite beyond practices now generally in effect. In particular, the "academic lock-step" would be broken.

These proposals imply a "model" of the student, and the model we prefer is one of "self-reliance," as once espoused by Emerson and followed by Eliot at Harvard—Eliot supported "liberty and variety in education" and "free electives" for students. We recognize that heavy stress on an approach of options and individual choices does have implications for the reduction of a sense of "community," for continuation of efforts to create a group of people with largely identical interests and experiences, but few campuses have this sense of community any longer.

For students to make good choices, they need to be faced by good options, have adequate information and advice available, be within a constructive environment, be guided by reasonable outer boundaries on what they can and cannot do. We have generally more confidence in self-determination under these conditions than in a rule by "bureaucratic centralism"; but mistakes will be made either way—neither approach is all good or all bad.

ASSISTING CHANGE

Changes, such as we have suggested, can be encouraged; the gap between ideas and application can be reduced.

Changes, such as we have suggested, can be encouraged; the gap between ideas and application can be reduced. We once proposed the creation of a National Foundation for Higher Education. A National Fund for the Improvement of Postsecondary Education, drawing on our proposal, has now been established. It has already received many applications. We similarly proposed the creation of such funds at the state level, and at least one state legislature (California) has before it a specific suggestion for action from one of its committees. We have proposed that each campus each year set aside 1 to 3 percent of its existing budget to be directed toward new endeavors; that an office be created, at least on larger campuses, concerned with the improvement of undergraduate education; that new ideas on campus be subject to trial before review rather than requiring review by faculty committees (and often rejection) before trial; and that students be more involved in decision making in areas of special interest to them.

Change, of course, may not always be constructive.

Change, of course, may not always be constructive. We are concerned, particularly, with four possibilities:

1   That the competition for students, which will be most intense in the 1980s, may lead some institutions to lower their academic standards and even to have no standards at all. But, we believe, this will not be an unlimited possibility. Most students want a good education; nearly all parents want their children to receive a good education (aside from a few who just want a way out of their own moral responsibility); and most employers want graduates with a "solid" degree.

2   That pressure for equality of academic rewards from some students and faculty members may also press down on academic standards.

3　That the more intensive job hunt by students may lead to excessive vocationalism and to undue shifting from one field to another in constantly attempted adjustment to changing opportunities—an erratic pursuit curve.

4　That research funds may be too much directed, as is now the tendency at the federal level, to applied projects with anticipated early payoffs, and that this may draw faculty research attention unduly away from more basic research.

The most important single issue about change, however, is whether it will come primarily from internal leadership or whether it will be imposed more totally from external sources.

The most important single issue about change, however, is whether it will come primarily from internal leadership or whether it will be imposed more totally from external sources. The ability of universities "to initiate their own adaptations to society" is highly desirable "but the resistances are very great." However, they may be in real trouble "if the inertia is so great that change has to be imposed from the outside" (Ashby, 1967). We greatly favor internal initiative as the basic pattern of change. This is why we have argued for the selection of "activist" presidents—presidents who will give forward-looking leadership, for increased input from student sources into decision-making processes, for effective boards of trustees, and for the releasing of individual faculty initiative from undue prior restraints, as in advance approval of experiments.

When change does come from the outside, it is better that it arrive, as it has historically, by way of the suggestion of new ideas, of inquiry about possibilities, of new money encouraging new departures, and of establishment of new endeavors, rather than by way of edict, line-item budgets, or specific regulation We recognize, of course, that many favorable changes, such as the land-grant movement and the ending of racial discrimination, have given strong external encouragement, and that there will be similar occasions requiring external initiatives in the future.

Higher education should take the initiative in determining its own future.

Higher education needs to keep active, to keep growing, to keep on testing out the new and reevaluating the old. Higher education should take the initiative in determining its own future. When all is said and done, however, more change is likely to take place on the periphery of higher education—in nontraditional programs and in further education—than in colleges and universities themselves.

ACHIEVEMENT OF MORE EFFECTIVE GOVERNANCE

CHAPTER

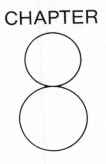

The governance of higher education in the United States in the 1960s experienced two great "shocks":

THE "STUDENT SHOCK"

For the first time in history, students, on a major scale, tried to assert their own "power" over the inner sanctum of academic and administrative affairs and to use the campus as a base for political action against elements of the surrounding society. Students in the past had confined themselves more largely to the running of extracurricular activities, and to individual and small group dissent. The most massive student confrontation by far ever to take place occurred in May 1970. A central theme of the leaders was reconstitution of the university and of society.

THE "CONTROL SHOCK"

Nearly all states now have coordinating councils or super-boards, with added powers, and more than half of all students and faculty members in public institutions are located on campuses within multicampus systems. Far more power is now concentrated at levels above the individual campus, perhaps in the order of a doubling in a single decade.

The miracle, however, is not that these shocks occurred in a nation where students had been viewed as "apathetic" and campuses as "autonomous," but that higher education survived so well and with so few changes at the operating levels of departments and schools. There have been "strong signs of internal stability" (Gross & Grambsch, forthcoming). Higher education has been greatly reorganized —in Germany, with tripartite rule in a number of states; in France, with decentralization and co-determination, although more in theory than in practice; in Japan, with new legal powers by the central government to reduce faculty salaries and to close campuses that are the subject of disruption. But not in the United States: more students sit on more committees and many faculty members are unhappy with the time and argument this involves, and more administrators are more frustrated by more bureaucratic layers imposed upon them from above, but little else has changed. Few states have passed any new laws specifically regulating campus conduct, and most states have passed none at all. The verbal fury has been greater than the legislative fact. There have been

The governance of higher education in the United States in the 1960s experienced two great "shocks."

The miracle, however, is not that these shocks occurred in a nation where students had been viewed as "apathetic" and campuses as "autonomous," but that higher education survived so well and with so few changes.

strong signs, also, of external stability. American higher education in the 1960s demonstrated substantial endurance, flexibility, adaptability, and continuing vitality.

But new shocks may be in store.

But new shocks may be in store:

COLLECTIVE BARGAINING

Collective bargaining is now spreading rapidly, although its future course is quite unclear. It now covers about 15 percent of the professoriate, mostly in community colleges and in comprehensive colleges and universities; it has penetrated little as yet into liberal arts colleges and research universities. It can come, when it does, as a supplement to current forms of governance, if it is confined to bargaining over matters of compensation; or it can be a totally new form of governance, as in the Boston State contract, covering all decision-making processes. Half or more of faculty members, according to our studies, now favor collective bargaining, and also favor greater militancy in asserting faculty interests.

Half or more of faculty members, according to our studies, now favor collective bargaining, and also favor greater militancy in asserting faculty interests.

POLITICALIZATION

The process of politicalization has gone quite far in many German, French, and Japanese universities, as it had earlier in some Latin-American universities. During a recent period in the United States, 1969–1972, as our studies have shown, about one-fifth to one-third of the American professoriate has favored the taking of political positions by organized faculties, or in other ways has indicated an attitude of "dissensus" toward the political neutrality of the university or the democratic processes of society or both. More than half of the professoriate now on campus was recruited during the great expansion decade of the 1960s and this segment will be dominant in faculty councils until the year 2000—and the 1960s constituted a very unusual decade in American history with extremely divisive internal and external issues affecting the political orientation of a whole academic generation.

About one-fifth to one-third of the American professoriate has favored the taking of political positions by organized faculties, or in other ways has indicated an attitude of "dissensus" toward the political neutrality of the university or the democratic processes of society or both.

No period may ever again occur that will draw forth such intensive political interest on campus, although this seems highly unlikely. People do change their minds, although this is less likely when they are concentrated in self-confirming groups than if they are widely dispersed. Also, the campus is probably now in a better position to handle political dissensus than it was when taken by surprise in the 1960s. Additionally, campuses may be more united internally against the actuality and the likely prospect of even greater external control—drawn together in mutual defense.

Left faculty members, in particular, may have generally decided, as have several of their most prominent leaders, that campus political neutrality is the best protection of their own individual right to dissent.

Nevertheless, these qualifications considered, a base may now exist for more political dissensus on campus than has ever before been the situation in the United States. There are more intellectuals in the United States than ever before, they hold positions of greater influence, and the campus is more at the center of their activities. And some of them are alienated from the surrounding society. The development, consequently, of their political relations on campus and vis-à-vis the surrounding society is of greater import to both the campus and society than in earlier times.

RESURGENCE OF STUDENT ACTIVISM

Student movements have always been very volatile in degree of activity (from little to much), in direction of effort (from left to right), and in tactics (from persuasion to violence). The decade of the 1960s is an excellent illustration of this historical pattern of the rise and fall of student movements, and of the shifts in emphasis and on methods within them. It is highly possible that a new period of student activism will occur again in the future— it would be quite remarkable if it did not. But it seems to take several student generations between the collapse of one movement and the start of another. The students after May 1970, whether because of reaction against violence and factionalism, or because of disgust with society and with their own ineffectiveness, or because of any one of many other possible explanations, deserted activism except in the area of women's liberation. It may take some substantial time before new enthusiasm builds and new leaders arise, but, even then, any new activism will depend upon the issues of the day, and no one can yet know what they may be and when they may develop.

It is highly possible that a new period of student activism will occur again in the future—it would be quite remarkable if it did not.

GLACIAL SPREAD OF PUBLIC CONTROL

Control by federal and state governments continues to advance like a new ice age. Realization of the seeming inevitability of this advance, rather than its sudden occurrence, will constitute the shock, if indeed the glacial spread cannot be halted.

The 1970s may belong to faculty activism as the 1960s did to student activism.

Looking at the four sources of potential new initiatives described above, we conjecture that those originating with faculties, and particularly collective bargaining, may be the more dominant ones in the near future. The 1970s may belong to faculty activism as the 1960s did to student activism. The other major source may be additional public control. If initiative in the 1960s can be said to have belonged to students and to administrators as the major actors, it may currently be seen as belonging more instead to faculties and public authorities, the former seeking to protect past internal privileges and the latter seeking to advance future external interests.

THE THEORY AND PRACTICE OF GOVERNANCE

Higher education is inherently difficult to govern; so many different people and groups have so much interest in it, and it is such a complex entity. Moreover, there is no single clear principle of governance:[1]

1   To begin with, higher education is not a "government." It has no coercive power to collect taxes or enforce the law— power from which no one can escape. It is more a "service" that people can choose to obtain under certain conditions, and they can also choose to forgo it. Thus, for example, students have no inherent right to participate in governance on the grounds that no one should be governed compulsorily without being given a chance to join in the selection of those who will do the governing. There is no issue of the consent of the governed.

2   Nor does the doctrine of "interest" easily determine who should govern, for so many different people have so many different interests—students, faculty, alumni, trustees, among others.

[1] For a discussion of different theoretical bases for university governance, see Thompson (1972).

3   Nor does the doctrine of "competence" give unequivocal guidance, for competence varies greatly among groups and individuals depending upon the particular subject matter involved.

Neither the presence of any ultimate coercive control nor the principles of interest and competence create a clear basis for deciding who should govern. We have chosen, in our own discussions of the matter, to favor mixed forms of governance and to be concerned mostly with how the best decisions may be made. This, in turn, means concern for where responsibility and competence are located both generally and issue by issue; and, to a lesser extent, with who has an interest in the particular decisions made, with how assent may be obtained, and also, to a much lesser extent, with how the educative value of participation may be secured.

We have chosen, in our own discussions of the matter, to favor mixed forms of governance and to be concerned mostly with how the best decisions may be made and this, in turn, means concern for where responsibility and competence are located.

The governance of higher education, we believe, is more a matter of how good decisions can be made than it is one of any single clear principle to be followed. We have concluded, generally, that the structures of governance for higher education in the United States are adequate as they now exist, with the need for improvements rather than for basic reform. We favor:

We have concluded, generally, that the structures of governance for higher education in the United States are adequate as they now exist, with the need for improvements rather than for basic reform.

- Continuation of state responsibility for higher education, as against the creation of a national system as occurs in so many other countries; and maintenance of the degree of independence that private institutions have historically enjoyed.

- The exercise of state responsibility for coordination through broad instruments.

- The establishment of clear lines of demarcation between what belongs to the state and what belongs to higher education—we have sought to draw such lines.

- The distribution of state funds on the basis of general formulas and rewards for performance, rather than on the basis of line-item budgets and specific controls.

- The preservation (or creation) of strong and independent boards of trustees with basic responsibility for the welfare of institutions of higher education.

- The appointment of presidents prepared to give affirmative leadership, but such leadership, both as matter of principle and of necessity, must be based upon persuasion, not dictation.

■ The delegation of basic influence over academic matters to faculties.

■ The continuation of the principle of tenure, with modifications in practice to reduce its rigidities. Prospectively 90 percent of full-time faculty members may have tenure by 1990.

■ The granting to faculty members, where they do not now have it, of rights to collective bargaining by state law, with the strong hope that they will consider carefully the wisdom of its use in each particular situation. (There will be many situations, we believe, where resort to collective bargaining will not prove advantageous, on balance, to faculty members.) If bargaining does take place, we believe that it should be on the basis of a craft approach for faculty members in a unit by themselves, and of contracts that confine themselves to economic matters —to the extent that this may be possible—leaving academic matters to academic bodies.

■ The greater involvement of students in several ways, including service as voting members of selected committees along with faculty members or administrators or trustees, or in parallel committees that meet in consultation with faculty or administrative or trustee committees. But, we are opposed to their membership on boards of trustees and faculty senates at their own institutions for the several reasons we have elsewhere set forth.

■ The better preparation for emergency situations—including clarification of policies, of location of authority, of methods of action.

■ The development of better rules governing relationships and conduct. More specifically, we have suggested the general outlines of (1) an "Academic Constitution," of (2) a "Bill of Rights and Responsibilities for Members of the Campus Community," and of (3) a "Code of Teaching Responsibility." We place particular stress on the importance of the understandings that lie behind such documents, and on the necessity of having them in good order in advance of difficulties.

■ The distribution of federal, and also state funds, where reasonably possible, from several sources and through the support of individual projects and individual students. Reliance on several sources of funding, and on students and panels of experts as "markets," appeals to us because it reduces the likelihood of detailed governmental controls and of political interference, it opens up the possibility of more dynamic adjustments, it reduces the need for advance agreement on specific objectives, and it gives greater scope to individual preferences.

INDEPENDENCE AND FREEDOM

The United States has the great advantage of a decentralized system of administration of the responsibility for higher education through the 50 states and through hundreds of private institutions.

The United States has the great advantage of a decentralized system of administrative responsibility for higher education through the 50 states and through hundreds of private institutions, rather than organization in one national system; and of the participation of thousands of interested citizens on boards of trustees, rather than policy determination through external bureaucracies. These advantages should be preserved.

Our greatest single concern at the present time, however, is that in some states "superboards" and legislators and governors are now exercising too much detailed policy and administrative control over institutions of higher education and unduly infringing upon their essential independence, are neglecting higher education too much financially and controlling it too much administratively. They should, instead, support and advise. To reach a peak of effectiveness, higher education needs money and talent, but it also requires essential independence for its institutions and academic freedom for its members.

Institutional independence never has been total, nor should it be. Higher education also has never had less independence from public control, in all of American history, than it now has. More institutions of higher education are public than ever before. More public authority is now exercised over both public and private institutions also than ever before. The great change of the past decade was not the vociferous rise of student power but the quiet increase in public power—by governors, by legislators, by coordinating councils. Some of higher education already has the status of a highly controlled public utility.

The great change of the past decade was not the vociferous rise of student power but the quiet increase in public power. . . . Some of higher education already has the status of a highly controlled public utility.

Public control has increased for many reasons. More of higher education receives public support. More individuals are affected by the conduct of higher education. More national resources are spent on it. But public control has not only intruded into higher education for these and other reasons, it has also been, in effect, invited into higher education by disruption that calls for external intervention, by internal disputes taken into the courts, by collective bargaining that turns over to outside agencies determination of the composition of bargaining units and the subject matter coverage of agreements—essential elements of governance—by participation of institutional bodies in partisan politics, and by a lack of strong leadership at the institutional and organizational levels. Independence has been given away as much as it has been taken away. The gift is less understandable than the seizure.

Yet the campus needs a large measure of independence for its effective performance.

Yet the campus needs a large measure of independence for its effective performance—for the sense of freedom of its individual members, for the exercise of professional judgment in areas of professional competence, for the avoidance of political intrusion from the outside, for the sake of the flexible use of resources.

We have made two major suggestions about the preservation of institutional independence:

1   The need for an understanding of what belongs to public authority and what belongs to the campus; otherwise, independence tends to erode away bit by bit and year by year. (See our report on *Governance* for a suggested distribution of items for public control and for institutional independence.)

2   The advisability of distribution of public funds by way of individuals where reasonably possible—as in research funds on the merits of individual applications, and student aid and federal support of educational costs via students and not via institutions as corporate bodies. We favor more reliance on a "market model" for higher education and less on an intensification of the "public utility model."

Above all, however, higher education must continue to earn its independence by the excellence of its educational and research programs, the openness of its conduct, the avoidance of institutional participation in the arena of partisan politics, the academic integrity of its internal decisions on admissions, on appointments and promotions, on grades and degrees, the avoidance of a self-serving attitude. Institutional independence has always assumed a certain acceptable level of academic performance and a high degree of institutional restraint in the area of external politics.

Institutional independence has always assumed a certain acceptable level of academic performance and a high degree of institutional restraint in the area of external politics.

The academic freedom of individual members of the campus is by now much better protected by the law, by common consent, by the standards and actions of the American Association of University Professors than is institutional independence, but the price of academic freedom is eternal vigilance. We have two comments to make:

1   Academic freedom is now threatened internally as well as externally—by some ideological adherents within as well as by some holders of power without. Thus it becomes more important than ever before that judicial processes on the campus are fully independent of improper internal pressures and biases. Processes of faculty hearings established, in part, to protect faculty members from attacks by external powers must now also be capable of protecting the integrity of the campus against those who undertake internal attacks on academic freedom; they must be able to convict internal enemies of freedom as well as protect against external enemies; they must be able to make findings of the guilt as well as of the innocence of fellow faculty members. We have made suggestions on how to ensure the greater independence of the judicial process.

2   Faculty members should not be held to higher standards in their roles as citizens than are other citizens. "His special position in the community" should not impose, as the American Association of University Professors now recommends, "special obligations" on a faculty member in his role as a citizen.[2] This rule, intended to guide conduct, should be changed. Faculty members, concomitantly, should not be able to plead that their civil liberties as citizens are a basis for not meeting academic standards of conduct on campus. "Free speech" is not an excuse for inaccuracy as a scholar or misuse of the classroom as a teacher. Academic freedom means, among other things, the right to select research topics and to publish results, to determine course content and to teach it—subject to meeting academic standards of conduct, not just to staying within the bounds of legally permissible conduct of citizens in the streets. Faculty members as citizens should be able to act as citizens without imposed special obligations and, as faculty members, should be held to the highest standards of academic integrity and scholarship. The two roles have distinctive obligations and should not be confused with each other; as citizens, scholars should be held to the standards of citizenship and as scholars, to the standards of scholarship—no more and no less.

[2] See the discussion of this problem in Van Alstyne (1972).

Institutional independence and internal academic freedom do not guarantee an illustrious system of higher education, but without them the heights of eminence will never be reached.

Institutional independence and internal academic freedom do not guarantee an illustrious system of higher education, but without them the heights of eminence will never be reached.

In the 1970s as in the 1870s—both periods of more than normal change—two of the greatest conflicts in higher education are (and were) over control and over purpose. But some functions of higher education, particularly such "autonomous" functions as independent scholarship and critical dissent, are subject to conflict at nearly all times and in many places; academic governance cannot be expected to be an exercise in tranquility.

ASSURANCE OF RESOURCES AND THEIR MORE EFFECTIVE USE

CHAPTER

Higher education experienced in the 1960s an increase in its total resources greater than ever before in its history. It more than doubled its expenditures as a percentage of the GNP from 1.1 percent to 2.5 percent. This resulted from a doubling of students (from 3 to over 6 million on a full-time equivalent basis), an unusually rapid increase in cost per student per year—from the historical rate of the cost of living plus 2.5 percent to a new rate of plus about 3.4 percent (5.0 percent for private institutions), and a great augmentation in research expenditures.

These rates of increases could not continue indefinitely. Enrollments in the 1970s were recently expected to rise more nearly by 50 percent than by 100 percent. The increase in cost per student was seen as likely to rise more nearly at the general rate of inflation plus 2.5 percent, as it has done historically, or perhaps at the rate of 2.4 percent as we have recommended. Research expenditures were expected to move ahead with the rate of increase of the GNP, again as we have recommended, rather than at 10 to 15 percent a year as they did during much of the 1960s.

CURRENT PROBLEMS

All these recent predictions of continued growth, even though they were below the levels of the 1960s, have thus far proved to be too expansive. Enrollments are falling below projected levels and may rise by about one-third rather than by one-half over the decade (see Table 1). The increase in expenditures per student (for a representative list of 41 institutions) has been rising recently at the rate of only 0.5 percent per year more than the rise in the cost of living (Cheit, 1973)—far below the historical level. This is such a low rate of increase that it cannot be continued without grave consequences for quality.

Higher education does not lend itself very readily to permanent increases in productivity. Thus its rising costs, for salaries and for other expenditures, are directly reflected in the prices it must charge to public or private sources of funds, whereas in industrial sectors of the economy cost increases are offset by an average annual rate of increase in productivity of 2.5 percent. In this respect, higher education resembles some other service sectors of the economy, which also experience difficulty in achieving productivity increases. This is why, if quality is to be maintained and if salary increases are to match those

Higher education experienced in the 1960s an increase in its total resources greater than ever before in its history.

All these recent predictions of continued growth, even though they were below the levels of the 1960s, have thus far proved to be too expansive.

elsewhere, we must expect expenditures per student to rise as rapidly as the cost of living plus about 2.5 percent. The 0.5 percent rate cannot long be maintained without serious deterioration of quality or of comparative salary levels or, more likely, of both. And research expenditures are not rising as fast as the GNP—in fact they are falling in real terms and are being directed more toward applied topics rather than toward the basic research that the university is especially fitted to perform.

Continuation of current trends will have the most serious of consequences.

Continuation of current trends will have the most serious of consequences. Facilities for students, on the average, will become less adequate. Research quality will decline, and library resources will deteriorate. More conflict will arise on campus over the distribution of resources, and this conflict will be based more upon the organization of group power.

REMEDIES

The answers lie in the two-pronged search for better use of resources on the one hand and augmentation of resources on the other. To reduce costs, as compared with the trends of the 1960s, we earlier made a number of suggestions aimed at holding current fund institutional expenditures of higher education in 1980 to $41.5 billion (1970 dollars) or 2.7 percent of the GNP as compared with $51 billion (1970 dollars) or 3.3 percent of the GNP if the trends of the 1960s were to continue—a reduction of nearly 20 percent.[1] Once the danger appeared to be that higher education would fail to meet this savings mark of 20 percent; now the danger is that it may be forced to exceed it.

Once the danger appeared to be that higher education would fail to meet this savings mark of 20 percent; now the danger is that it may be forced to exceed it.

We have suggested as major ways of holding down the bill for higher education:

---

[1] Adjusting for new enrollment projections the figures are $37 billion and $46 billion, and the percentages are 2.4 and 3.0. If cost per student rises, as we have recommended, but the acceleration of programs, which we have also recommended, does not occur—and this is, perhaps, the most realistic possibility— the figures return to $41.5 billion and 2.7 percent of the GNP. We have in recent reports made certain suggestions which would add to costs on top of each of the figures given above: (1) $150 to $200 million per year to adjust salaries of women faculty members to those of men; (2) about $600 million per year for additional "nontraditional" students within higher education—see Projection III in Technical Note A; and (3) $50 or $60 million a year (aside from any capital costs) for "Learning Pavillions" as set forth in our recent report, *Toward a Learning Society*. In total, these would add about $1 billion to each of the foregoing amounts.

■ Withdrawal of the reluctant attenders, whom we estimated at 5 to 12 percent. Some of this apparently is happening already with the pressure of the draft on attendance removed, and for other reasons.

■ Introduction of shorter time options for students. This would save time for the students and expenditures for higher education, and reduce the duplication of about two-thirds of a year's work between high school and college with its impacts on the deteriorated morale of students—they get "turned off" by the waste and the boredom.

■ Augmentation of research expenditures at about the average annual rate of increase in the GNP rather than at a faster rate.

■ Great caution in the introduction of new Ph.D. programs.

■ Careful consideration of shifting to year-round operation where it is determined that this will achieve savings in operating and capital costs combined.

■ Elimination of unnecessary duplication of effort within and among institutions.

■ General attention to costs in all categories.

We also expect that the improvement of faculty salaries will be more nearly in accord with that of wages and salaries generally rather than rising much more rapidly as in the 1960s. Faculty salaries certainly should rise with the cost of living, and preferably should also rise with the productivity gains of the economy generally.

We are convinced that substantial savings—on the order of 20 percent—can be made as compared with continuation of the trends of the 1960s—without loss of quality, but no more than that can be done without long-term damage to a great national resource.

We are convinced that substantial savings—on the order of 20 percent—can be made as compared with continuation of the trends of the 1960s—without loss of quality, but no more than that can be done without long-term damage to a great national resource.

The other avenue is increased income.

We have suggested that the federal government absorb about one-half of the public share of total monetary outlays for higher education, particularly by providing a more adequate financing of equality of opportunity, by increasing research expenditures along with the rising level of the GNP, and by absorbing more of the costs of graduate training, particularly at the level of the M.D., D.D.S., and Ph.D.

The states, in addition, will need to raise their average contribution to about 1.0 percent of personal income[2] in order to provide facilities for the additional students, to offset the rising costs per student, to supplement the student aid available from the federal government, and to provide assistance for private institutions.

Tuition will need to rise, as we have recommended, at about the rate of increase in per capita disposable income (a rough index of ability to pay) at private institutions, unless they can achieve constructive economies that make possible smaller tuition increases. At public institutions, tuition will need to rise, on the average, substantially faster than this in order to narrow the recently widening tuition gap with private institutions and to provide more funds. We have suggested that public tuition, on the average, rise over the next decade to about one-third of educational costs as compared with the current one-sixth. There is, of course, a great sensitivity to rises in this "price," partly because it represents a big outlay all at once and partly also because some believe that it should be a "free" service, as it is in primary and secondary schools. All rises in tuition should be matched by increased aid to low-income students, and recent improvements in student-aid support at the state level make this now a more realistic possibility.

Philanthropy—from individuals, foundations, and business—is an important source of funds for many institutions; the conditions for its continuation must be preserved, and its importance must be more fully realized.

The institutions now in the greatest financial difficulty are (a) the great research universities, (b) the lesser-known private liberal arts colleges, and (c) the large, private comprehensive colleges and universities.

The institutions now in the greatest financial difficulty are (a) the great research universities, (b) the lesser-known private liberal arts colleges, and (c) the large, private comprehensive colleges and universities. Institutions in the first group provide much of the highest level skills and new ideas for American society, the second create much of the diversity within higher education, and the third have been major sources of opportunity for middle- and lower-income students in a number of metropolitan areas. (See Tables 2 and 3 for data on the major component parts of higher education.)

[2] The level in 1967–68 was about 0.74 percent, and currently is about 0.90 percent. See Appendix Table 6 and Appendix Chart 2 for the record of state support in terms of percent of personal income. The record is one of steady growth except for World War II. The long upward climb of this percentage is approaching a plateau.

To obtain the greater public support needed in the future, higher education must demonstrate to the satisfaction of the public that its purposes are essential, that is governance is effective, and that it makes good use of the resources available to it.

To obtain the greater public support needed in the future, higher education must demonstrate to the satisfaction of the public that its purposes are essential, that its governance is effective, and that it makes good use of the resources available to it. Not only has higher education lost a degree of public support in recent years, but it is now in a more competitive position vis-à-vis other national priorities.

At best, higher education can hope to return to the historic level of rising expenditures per student. It cannot expect a return to the conditions of the 1960s for the foreseeable future.

TABLE 1   Higher education: increases in enrollments, in expenditures per student, in institutional expenditures and as a percentage of the GNP, and in federal research expenditures, 1960, 1970, 1980

	1960	1960 to 1970	1970	1970 to 1980	1980
1. INCREASES IN ENROLLMENT					
a. FTE ENROLLMENTS (THOUSANDS)	3,000		6,800		8,800*
b. AVERAGE ANNUAL RATE OF INCREASE		8.5		2.6	
c. CUMULATIVE PERCENTAGE INCREASE		126.7		29.7	
2. AVERAGE ANNUAL RATE OF INCREASE IN TOTAL CURRENT FUND EXPENDITURES PER FTE STUDENT OVER AND ABOVE THE GENERAL RISE IN THE COST OF LIVING:					
a. HISTORIC RATE OF INCREASE, 1930–1960	2.5				
b. TREND OF 1960s		3.4			
c. PROVIDED EXPERIENCE OF 1970–1973 CONTINUES				0.5	
d. AS RECOMMENDED BY THE CARNEGIE COMMISSION				2.4	
3. TOTAL CURRENT FUND EXPENDITURES OF INSTITUTIONS IN BILLIONS (1970–1971 DOLLARS):					
a. ACTUAL	$8.4		$24.2		
(1) AVERAGE ANNUAL RATE OF INCREASE		11.2			
(2) PERCENT OF GNP	1.1		2.5		
b. ENROLLMENT PROJECTION I†					
(1) ESTIMATED TOTAL WITH CONTINUATION OF 1960 TO 1970 TREND IN CURRENT FUND EXPENDITURES PER FTE STUDENT					$50.8

TABLE 1   (continued)

	1960	1960 to 1970	1970	1970 to 1980	1980
(2) AVERAGE ANNUAL RATE OF INCREASE				7.7	
(3) PERCENT OF GNP					3.3
(4) ESTIMATED TOTAL AS RECOMMENDED BY CARNEGIE COMMISSION WITH ACCELERATED PROGRAMS AND OTHER EFFICIENCY GAINS					$41.4
(5) AVERAGE ANNUAL RATE OF INCREASE				5.5	
(6) PERCENT OF GNP					2.7
c. ENROLLMENT PROJECTION II					
(1) ESTIMATED TOTAL WITH CONTINUATION OF 1960 TO 1970 TREND IN CURRENT EXPENDITURES PER FTE STUDENT					$45.8
(2) AVERAGE ANNUAL RATE OF INCREASE				6.6	
(3) PERCENT OF GNP					3.0
(4) ESTIMATED TOTAL AS RECOMMENDED BY CARNEGIE COMMISSION WITH EFFICIENCY GAINS BUT *WITHOUT* ACCELERATED PROGRAMS					41.5
(5) AVERAGE ANNUAL RATE OF INCREASE				5.5	
(6) PERCENT OF GNP					2.7
(7) ESTIMATED TOTAL AS RECOMMENDED BY CARNEGIE COMMISSION *WITH* ACCELERATED PROGRAMS AND OTHER EFFICIENCY GAINS					$37.3
(8) AVERAGE ANNUAL RATE OF INCREASE				4.4	
(9) PERCENT OF GNP					2.4
4. FEDERAL RESEARCH EXPENDITURES THROUGH HIGHER EDUCATION IN MILLIONS (1958 DOLLARS)	$380		$1,180		
a. AVERAGE ANNUAL RATE OF INCREASE OVER AND ABOVE THE GENERAL RISE IN THE COST OF LIVING		12.0			
b. AT ACTUAL RATE OF 1968–1972				—2.1	
c. AS RECOMMENDED BY THE CARNEGIE COMMISSION				4.2	

*Projection II, Technical Note A.

†See Technical Note A and our report, *The More Effective Use of Resources.*

TABLE 2   Enrollment in institutions of higher education and number of institutions, by type of institution and control, United States, 1970

TYPE OF INSTITUTION	ENROLLMENT (IN THOUSANDS)					NUMBER OF INSTITUTIONS				
	PUBLIC	PRIVATE	TOTAL	PER-CENT PUBLIC	PER-CENT OF TOTAL	PUBLIC	PRIVATE	TOTAL	PER-CENT PUBLIC	PER-CENT OF TOTAL
TOTAL*	6,364.4	2,132.0	8,496.2	74.9	100.0	1,313	1,514	2,827	46.4	100.0
DOCTORAL-GRANTING INSTITUTIONS	1,900.8	636.9	2,537.7	74.9	29.9	101	63	164	61.6	5.8
HEAVY EMPHASIS ON RESEARCH	774.3	236.5	1,010.8	76.6	11.9	26	20	46	56.5	1.6
MODERATE EMPHASIS ON RESEARCH	579.2	155.1	734.5	78.9	8.6	30	18	48	62.5	1.7
MODERATE EMPHASIS ON DOCTORAL PROGRAMS	278.8	135.6	414.4	67.3	4.9	23	12	35	65.7	1.2
LIMITED EMPHASIS ON DOCTORAL PROGRAMS	268.5	109.7	378.2	71.0	4.5	22	13	35	62.9	1.2
COMPREHENSIVE COLLEGES	2,109.9	533.6	2,643.4	79.8	31.1	316	147	463	68.3	16.4
COMPREHENSIVE COLLEGES I	1,679.6	411.5	2,091.1	80.3	24.6	210	91	301	69.8	10.6
COMPREHENSIVE COLLEGES II	430.3	122.1	552.3	77.9	6.5	106	56	162	65.4	5.7
LIBERAL ARTS COLLEGES	34.8	643.9	678.6	5.1	8.0	27	676	703	3.8	24.9
SELECTIVITY I	0.0	156.5	156.5	0.0	1.8	0	121	121	0.0	4.3
SELECTIVITY II	34.8	487.4	522.1	6.7	6.1	27	555	582	4.6	20.6
TWO-YEAR INSTITUTIONS	2,214.0	133.8	2,347.8	94.3	27.6	805	256	1,061	75.9	37.5
SPECIALIZED INSTITUTIONS	104.9	183.6	288.5	36.4	3.4	64	372	436	14.7	15.4

* Excludes extension enrollment separately reported by institutions; items may not add to totals because of rounding.

SOURCE: Adapted from U.S. Office of Education data by the Carnegie Commission staff.

TABLE 3   Current fund expenditures,* by institutions of higher education, by type and control, estimated 1970–71 (in billions of current dollars)

TYPE OF INSTITUTION	PUBLIC		PRIVATE		ALL INSTITUTIONS	
	AMOUNT	PERCENT OF TOTAL	AMOUNT	PERCENT OF TOTAL	AMOUNT	PERCENT OF TOTAL
UNIVERSITIES	9.7	63.0	4.8	54.5	14.5	59.9
OTHER FOUR-YEAR INSTITUTIONS	3.6	23.4	3.8	43.2	7.4	30.6
TWO-YEAR INSTITUTIONS	2.1	13.6	0.2	2.3	2.3	9.5
TOTAL	15.4	100.0	8.8	100.0	24.2	100.0

* Includes all current fund expenditures, except current funds expended for physical plant assets.

SOURCES: USOE/NCES, *Projections of Educational Statistics to 1980–81,* U.S. Government Printing Office, Washington, D.C., 1972, pp. 96–97; composition was estimated by projecting expenditures forward for three years on the basis of (1) changes in total enrollment by type (see USOE/NCES, *Opening Fall Enrollment in Higher Education 1970, Report on Preliminary Survey,* 1970, p. 10, and *Opening Fall Enrollment in Higher Education 1967,* p. 7), and (2) cumulations of annual average rates of increases in educational costs per credit hour for the three-year period, based on 1953–54 to 1966–67 experience (see *The More Effective Use of Resources,* p. 34). These independent projections by type were then adjusted to the estimated figures for public, private, and total.)

CONCLUSION ON PRIORITIES

CHAPTER

Higher education has held a preferred place in private and public priorities in the United States. This can be seen not only in public opinion polls over the years but even better in actions actually taken. Most parents want their children to go to college. Many students do go to college when they have reasonable access. When individual citizens have more money to spend, they tend to spend it disproportionately on higher education— the income elasticity of demand appears to be above unity, which means that with a 1 percent increase in income there will be more than a 1 percent increase in private expenditures on higher education. Taxpayers, through their legislators, have also shown a propensity to direct additional expenditures strongly toward higher education. The American people in the 1960s, as a result of both private and public decisions, more than doubled their expenditures on higher education as compared with expenditures on all other goods and services combined. Behind these enrollment propensities and expenditure rates lie convictions that higher education serves great purposes for individuals and society.

These convictions of the worth of higher education have been shaken somewhat in recent years. We have proposed, above, six priorities for higher education in the expectation that their fulfillment can both restore these convictions to their earlier levels and lead higher education to a greater sense of its own value. The accomplishment of each priority will serve both society and higher education.

We recognize some conflicts among these priorities; not all good things are consistent with one another. For example, program enrichment costs money, but money must be conserved, and an effort at clarification of purposes may make governance, at least temporarily, more difficult as fundamental issues are raised for discussion. But we believe, nevertheless, that each of these six priorities is essential in its own right and is capable of realization simultaneously with the others. As a result of their accomplishment, higher education will be accorded a more highly preferred place in the estimation of the people and of its own direct participants.

We end this discussion of priorities, however, by noting that, viewed in their entirety, we place an equal or even greater priority on assistance to preschool education and to urban-center high schools. These segments of formal education affect more people, and improvement in them is no less essential.

Higher education has held a preferred place in private and public priorities in the United States.

These convictions of the worth of higher education have been shaken somewhat in recent years.

Each of these six priorities is essential in its own right and is capable of realization simultaneously with the others.

FUTURE
POSSIBILITIES

THE CONSTANTLY CHANGING SCENE: THE EXPERIENCE OF THE CARNEGIE COMMISSION

CHAPTER

11

Higher education has been going through a period of many discontinuities, of many new impacts from many directions. The history of the Carnegie Commission illustrates this. The Commission was first planned in 1966. The original intention was to concentrate on financial problems because it was already then apparent that rapidly rising enrollments and rising costs per student would be the sources of a troublesome augmentation of costs as against prospective revenues. It was decided, however, that a study of financing should be combined with a broader consideration of how the new financial problems were being brought about, and what some of their repercussions might be. The main theme thus started out to be the impact of universal access to higher education, its financial costs, and its impacts on functions, on governance, and on academic innovations. Universal access is a phenomenon of great historic impact and has been a central concern of the Commission from start to finish.

But new concerns quickly arose, and the Commission added them into its agenda.

STUDENT UNREST

By June of 1967, when the Commission held its first organizational meeting, there had been several major student disruptions, but this was before the developments at Columbia, Harvard, and Cornell, and the great nationwide outburst in May 1970, which included the killings at Kent State and Jackson State.

NEEDS FOR HEALTH CARE PERSONNEL

Health care demands began rising at an accelerated rate, and so did health care costs. A shortage of health care personnel became increasingly evident. Higher education was the main source of training for such personnel; it had grave responsibilities to meet the new needs.

THE CHANGING LABOR MARKET

Job opportunities for college graduates began turning downward in 1968, and a lack of active demand continued until 1973. A new period had arrived when, short-term fluctuations aside, the supply of college graduates would more than meet the demands for them in jobs customarily held by college graduates.

Higher education has been going through a period of many discontinuities, of many new impacts from many directions.

COLLECTIVE BARGAINING

Unionization of college faculties began to spread for the first time in history, and collective bargaining potentially could have a major impact on higher education, as earlier on American industry.

WOMEN'S LIBERATION MOVEMENT

Women began demanding more access to graduate school and to faculty positions. Historically largely on the periphery of higher education, aside from a few fields like teacher training and social welfare, they now began asking for more central roles across-the-board. The ancient universities had been entirely male preserves. A basic transformation was begun.

RISING INTEREST IN THE WELFARE OF THE TOTAL POSTSECONDARY AGE GROUP

As nearly half and then prospectively more than half of this age group enters higher education, the situation of those outside— of those unsubsidized and unassisted—becomes of more interest. The Commission became increasingly concerned with the welfare of this segment of youth, as it believes American society will also come to be. How can young persons of all talents and family incomes best be aided in getting a fair educational start into life and work? What should be done for the "outs" as well as for the "ins"?

THE SHIFT OF INITIATIVE TO THE STATES

The Great Society quickly gave way to the New Federalism, with attention shifting from what the federal government might do for higher education back to what the states would do. A corollary of this was a shift from high concern on the part of government for equality of opportunity to more concern for what each person could do to take care of himself.

Several new developments occurred at about the same time, the most basic one being the advent of universal access.

Thus, several new developments occurred at about the same time, the most basic one being the advent of universal access; but each of the others also had substantial significance. Higher education, after two decades of triumphs, found itself suddenly surrounded by problems, drawn into a maelstrom of controversies.

There will certainly be other new developments in the future to engage the attention of higher education. Three now interest us in particular:

NEW ENROLLMENT PATTERNS

Here is the one major area where we wish to reconsider our earlier predictions and recommendations.

One is the prospect of changing enrollment patterns. Here is the one major area where we wish to reconsider our earlier predictions and recommendations (see Chart 4 and Technical Note A). We were among the first to call attention several years ago to the 1980s as a "stop" period after a century when enrollments had doubled every 10 to 15 years. But we did not anticipate that the declining rate of enrollment increases would occur so soon and so fast in the 1970s or that the 1990s might turn out to be such a period of continuing slow growth in enrollments, as now seems possible. We expected a new surge ahead beginning about 1990—a new "go" period. We spoke of "new uncertainties" when we were making our earlier predictions, but we did not expect they would come so soon or be so uncertain. The upward rate of enrollment ratios among white males has turned down at least temporarily, and the birthrate has dropped drastically, among other factors.

Consequently we would now caution greater conservatism in planning for new campuses or in expanding old campuses or in undertaking new construction than we evidenced in our own recommendations even two years ago. We would also advise more efforts by colleges to bring in part-time and "recurrent" students in order both to make good use of college facilities and to extend service to such students. It is possible that the gap between our earlier predictions and our current ones could be filled in significant part by the addition of such "nontraditional" students. We note that colleges with "protected" markets in the past—protected by religious affiliations or by local affection— may suffer the most if enrollment levels fade. Prospective levels for total expenditures for higher education will, of course, decline with any decline in prospective enrollments.

Demographic changes have had a very major impact on the American educational system in recent times. High marriage and birth rates after World War II reduced college attendance by women; then the higher postwar birthrate flooded, in turn, elementary, secondary, and tertiary schools; then it resulted in a sharp increase in new entrants to the labor market; along the way, it led to the recruitment of more than half of current faculty members in a single decade; later, it will result in a great upsurge in faculty retirements. Now this is all being reversed, and women are going to college in larger numbers and expecting to be advanced more in academic life, enrollments are falling off in elementary and secondary schools and soon also in higher education, and so forth. Massive demographic irregularities have had massive impacts on education, including higher education.

NEW MENTALITIES

A second new development, or at least a potential new development, is changing mentalities among the participants in higher education (and in society). We have earlier referred to the dissensus that has developed within the American professoriate over the political role of the university. A similar dissensus has developed among students. There appears to be a sudden elevation among significant numbers of faculty members and students of the doctrine of political commitment within the conduct of academic life—commitment to institutional action in political disputes, even to acceptance of disruption as a form of political action.

But other new mentalities may also be arising: a new interest in the affective and the sensate, a new refusal to enter into competition in college and out, and an effort to press instead for a society organized more on horizontal than on pyramidal, meritocratic lines. Emphases on political commitment, on the sensate, on a completely egalitarian society are different from each other, and each also is different from the competitive "work ethic" and concentration on cognitive activity within the existing society on which higher education in the United States traditionally has been largely based.

Emphases on political commitment, on the sensate, on a completely egalitarian society are different from each other, and each also is different from the competitive "work ethic" and concentration on cognitive activity within the existing society on which higher education in the United States has been largely based.

How each of these competing mentalities may develop, we do not know, but the almost complete dominance of the older mentality that included emphases on full political neutrality, on the cognitive efforts of the mind, on stiff academic competition can no longer be so taken for granted by higher education. We are also concerned with the inevitable impact of a more meritocratic society in creating more "sliders," more students who accept or even insist upon a lower socioeconomic status than their parents. "Sliding" can be a painful experience for the individuals involved. And some campuses may need to adjust to the special problems of such students—they have been more oriented toward the climbers.

ABSORPTION OF WOMEN AND MINORITIES

A third new development, with as yet uncertain results, is "affirmative" action, the effort to place more women and members of minority groups in student bodies at all levels and on faculties. "Normal" expectations, with equality of opportunity, might be that about 38 percent of faculty members eventually might be women, and about 15 percent might be members of minority groups (the proportions they now form of the total labor force; among minorities—about 10 percent are blacks, about 4 percent are of Spanish origin, and about 1 percent are Asians and native Americans). Current figures are slightly more than half of this labor force rate for women (22.5 percent), and about one-third of this labor force rate for minorities (5.3 percent). (See Chart 5 and Technical Note B.)

A rapid closing of the two gaps is difficult for several reasons, including the reduced rate of new hires as compared with the 1960s (affirmative action might be said to have arrived on the scene 10 years too late), the insufficient numbers of qualified women and minorities now in the various subject matter pools available for employment, and the reduced opportunities for majority males who are already in general oversupply at the Ph.D. level. Our Commission opposes fixed numerical percentages for the hiring of women and minorities as a means of closing the two gaps. We do favor, however, strong efforts to increase the pools of qualified women and minorities and special consideration in hiring for women and minorities where their roles as models for students and their special sensitivities to the problems of women and minority students will add to the overall excellence of a department, school, or college.

Reasonable expectations for 1990 may be about 30 percent of faculties composed of women and nearly 9 percent of members of minorities. This will still leave gaps between these figures and normal expectations. It may take until the year 2000, or even beyond, before the levels of normal expectations for the inclusion of women and members of minority groups in the American professoriate are generally reached. (For normal expectations to be realized by the year 2000, the hiring rate

It may take until the year 2000, or even beyond, before the levels of normal expectations for the inclusion of women and members of minority groups in the American professoriate are generally reached.

for majority males would need to drop to one-third of all new hires in the 1990s. This may not be either reasonable or possible. It was about three-fourths of all hires in the 1960s.)

Each of the next three decades will have its own special problems: the 1970s—the small pools of qualified women and members of minority groups in most subject matter areas; the 1980s—the very low rate of all new hires; and the 1990s—the heavy proportion of women and minorities among new hires if normal expectations are to be reached by 2000.

There are many unknowns, including how much frustration may develop over this slow pace in closing the gaps and how much pressure may be exerted to close them more rapidly; and how much frustration may develop among majority males and how much pressure may be exerted to preserve opportunities for them. In any event, the problem of the absorption of women and minorities into faculties will be a troublesome one, with uncertain outcomes, for the duration of the twentieth century. While we hope and expect that very major progress will occur, we are opposed to efforts at precise, "fine-tuning," department-by-department actions. But the greatest uncertainty is whether a relatively full solution to the problem can wait until the year 2000.

And there will be some largely unanticipated new developments, as there have been since this Commission first began to meet in 1967. American higher education and American society are in an unusual state of flux.

Planning for the future of higher education should be on a contingent basis.

Thus planning for the future of higher education should be on a contingent basis, subject to constant reexamination. Such planning will be more useful when undertaken for the short term rather than for the long term and when based on broad considerations rather than on narrow, quantifiable factors alone. The technocratic planning analysts are bound to be proved wrong.

Constant study is required. Our own studies have been paralleled by several concurrent studies, and it is remarkable how so many of them have reached much the same conclusions about the essential problems in the current situation.

Constant study is required. Our own studies have been paralleled by several concurrent studies, and it is remarkable how so many of them have reached much the same conclusions about the essential problems in the current situation, and how so many of them have determined upon much the same recommendations for action, although degree of emphasis and rating of priorities vary substantially. All these contemporary studies follow upon earlier studies which, with a few exceptions, have pointed along much the same continuing paths of historical development. (For a discussion of these earlier and concurrent studies see Technical Note C.)

It is interesting to note, in going back over these reports to the Zook Commission in 1947, what has not been done, what has been done, and what has been overdone in relation to the recommendations earlier made. The Zook Commission, which was considered radical at the time, now appears—26 years later— quite in line with the current status quo. How may the more radical, or at least more progressive, study recommendations of today look 26 years hence in the year 2000? And more studies will be needed and made in the future as the situation keeps on changing, as new stages on the paths of historical development are reached.

Our own tactical approach to the examination of higher education and to recommendations about its future has had several elements.

Our own tactical approach to the examination of higher education and to recommendations about its future has had several elements.

■ The very *careful selection of topics* on which to report. We considered several times as many topics as we finally settled upon for study.

■ The *issuance of reports one at a time* so that each might better be targeted toward action and more easily be absorbed into thought than if they were all to be combined into one single voluminous report with several hundred recommendations.

■ The *selective timing of the issuance of reports.* We were successful in the timing of some, such as the reports on federal aid to higher education and on health manpower legislation— the reports on these subjects came out shortly before deliberations were reaching the point of administrative and legislative action, and each of these reports had a clear impact on policy formation at the federal level. We were unsuccessful on others, particularly our report on student unrest, which appeared in the spring of 1971 after the peak of student unrest and after the appearance of the Scranton Commission report the prior fall. Also, the two reports were quite similar in their approaches to policy.

■ The effort to make *specific recommendations.* We decided early to be specific in what we said so that others could agree or disagree, to avoid sole recourse to generalizations that led nowhere. In the course of this, we proved, sometimes, to be specifically wrong as well as right.

■ The search for *new data* where it would be helpful. Thus we looked at:

Prospective enrollments for the 1980s *(New Students and New Places)* and discovered that a great discontinuity in historical development was lying ahead for higher education.

Student and faculty opinion (The Carnegie Commission Survey of Student and Faculty Opinion) and found, among many other things, (a) that students were much more satisfied with their college experiences than was then publicly recognized—the revolutionary finding that no revolution was desired, and (b) that more political dissensus existed within the professoriate than had earlier been considered, by most observers, to be the situation; that students were happier and faculty members more divided than commonly thought.

The record of productivity changes in higher education (O'Neill, 1971) —a most important long-run factor—and found that there were none that could be measured.

Surveys of the plans and expectations of institutions with regard to graduate and professional education (Mayhew, 1970).

A survey of the opinions and expectations of public officials in nine states toward higher education (Eulau & Quinley, 1970).

Trends and projections of physicians in the United States (Blumberg, 1971).

The findings of a quarter-century of social science research on the influence of college attendance on people (Withey et al, 1971).

The impact of the expansion of college enrollment since 1900 on the average mental ability of college students (Taubman & Wales, 1972).

The sources of funds to colleges and universities (O'Neill, 1973).

The findings of economic research on the influence of college attendance on the lives of people (Juster, forthcoming).

The specific financial circumstances of representative colleges and universities (Cheit, 1971 & 1973).

The growing homogenization of colleges (Hodgkinson, 1971).

The events of May 1970 (Peterson & Bilorusky, 1971).

The opinions of young alumni about their college experiences (Spaeth & Greeley, 1970)

and at a number of other areas where new and better data could be useful to understanding.[1]

[1] For a summary of each of these and other studies undertaken for the Commission, see *Research Reports of the Carnegie Commission on Higher Education,* forthcoming.

There has been too much excessive, almost paralyzing, criticism.

■ The attempt to *see the situation as it really is.* The tendency of the age is to be excessively critical, to see failure in everything, to believe that nothing works. We found much to be wrong, but we also found much to be right in higher education— that more is right than is wrong; that higher education was not as far "down" and forever as currently thought, just as it was not as far "up" and forever as earlier had been considered to be the case. There has been recently too much excessive, almost paralyzing, criticism.

■ The effort to view the needs of *public and private higher education with equal interest* and sympathy, to avoid the dichotomy of public versus private institutions.

■ The effort to direct *recommendations to those who can act* upon them.

The real achievements lie with those who act effectively.

Studies have been and can be helpful. Effective action is essential. The real achievements lie with those who act effectively.

CHART 4   Total enrollments of students in higher education, actual to 1970, and estimated for 1980, 1990, 2000.

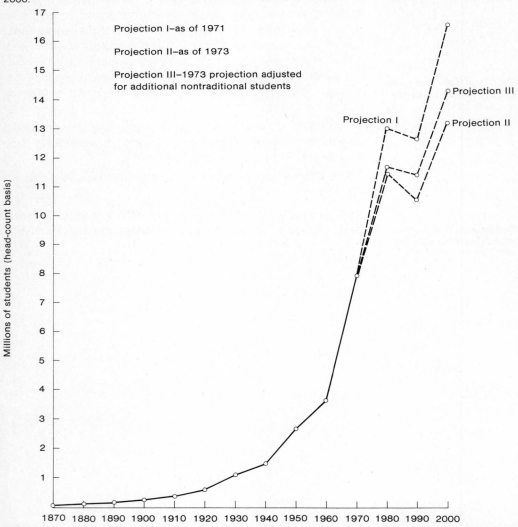

Projection I–as of 1971

Projection II–as of 1973

Projection III–1973 projection adjusted
for additional nontraditional students

SOURCE: See Technical Note A and Appendix B, *New Students and New Places.*   Enrollment data prior to 1960 exclude non-degree-credit enrollment.

CHART 5   Absorption of women and minorities into faculties

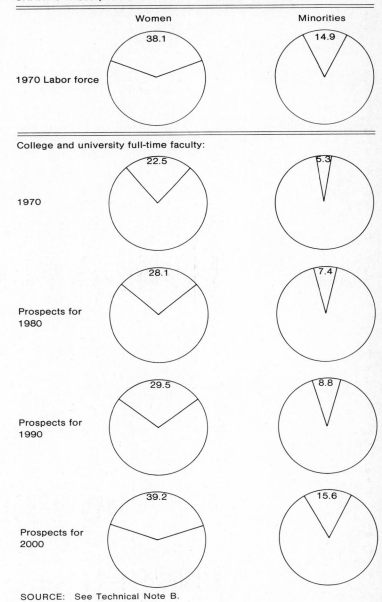

SOURCE: See Technical Note B.

WHO SHOULD DO WHAT? THE RECOMMEN- DATIONS OF THE CARNEGIE COMMISSION

CHAPTER

Throughout American history, first the colonies and then the states have been the main guardians of higher education through their laws, their policies, and their financial support. That they have done well in their guardianship is demonstrated by the diversity, vigor, and occasional excellence of the system of higher education in the United States. We strongly support the continuation of basic reliance on the states.

THE STATES

We have made a number of suggestions to the *states* about the future conduct of their guardianship:

■ They should provide an adequate number of places for students, particularly places of the open-access type and especially in metropolitan areas where the greatest deficits now exist. We have found a few states, however, to be quite derelict in fulfilling their responsibilities. (See Appendix Tables 4 and 5 for a listing of deficits by states and metropolitan areas as of recent dates. Some of these deficits have been overcome since these tables were prepared in connection with earlier reports. The new enrollment projections we are now making do not generally affect the listings of deficits of certain types of campuses because the basic criterion was geographical coverage. Sufficient places exist at or could be added to established campuses if they were ideally located and entirely of the needed types, which they are not.)

■ They should provide the public funds essential for the institutional support of both public and private institutions; we have estimated that the states (along with local jurisdictions) must be prepared to spend an average of about 1.0 percent of per capita income on state support of higher education for the rest of this decade, as compared with an estimated 1972–73 figure of about 0.90, if the new students still coming along are to be accommodated, if the rising costs are to be met, if the goal of equality of opportunity for students from low-income families is to be accomplished, and if private colleges are to be properly assisted. Many states now fall below this level of contribution. This figure of about 1.0 assumes a substantial increase in federal support. (See Appendix Table 6 and Appendix Chart 2 for the record of state support in terms of percentage of personal income.)

We strongly support the continuation of basic reliance on the states.

We have found a few states, however, to be quite derelict in fulfilling their responsibilities.

The states must be prepared to spend an average of about 1.0 percent of per capita income on state support of higher education for the rest of this decade.

The states should exercise restraint in the application of their potentially great powers and to this end should be prepared to agree with higher education on the outer boundaries of state control.

■ The states should exercise restraint in the application of their potentially great powers and to this end should be prepared to agree with higher education on the outer boundaries of state control. We have suggested limits to the intrusion of state power into the affairs of higher education.

■ They should provide for the effective coordination of postsecondary education, including emphasis on differentiation of functions among institutions, on diversity and specialization among and within institutions, on innovation, and on development of a whole series of educational channels for young persons seeking to enter work and adult life. No single state is now fully effective in its approach to coordination.

THE FEDERAL GOVERNMENT

The federal government has taken an ever-increasing interest in higher education since the Civil War and particularly since World War II. Over the past 30 years the federal government has been the single greatest new force affecting the course of development of higher education in the United States. We have proposed that the *federal government,* as it further evolves its role in relation to higher education, do the following:

Over the past 30 years the federal government has been the single greatest new force affecting the course of development of higher education in the United States.

■ Take basic responsibility for providing equality of opportunity through financial aid to students by way of improved programs for Basic Opportunity Grants, work-study, and loans, and for encouraging the states to supplement its efforts. Great steps forward were made in the 1960s and particularly in the Higher Education Act of 1972. Creation of a National Student Loan Bank is an essential addition to existing programs.

■ Continue major responsibility for supporting university research, and particularly basic research—on a steady basis— and assume more responsibility for financing graduate programs at the level of the Ph.D., the D.A., the M.D., and the D.D.S.

■ Expand responsibility for financing innovation through the National Fund for the Improvement of Postsecondary Education and the National Institute of Education.

■ Increase interest in the welfare of the total postsecondary age group by expanding, on an experimental basis, national service programs, and by improving educational opportunities in the military services, among other ways, and by studying the future possibility of an "educational endowment" for adults of all ages.

The federal government should be prepared to pay about half of the total monetary outlays for higher education that are paid from public sources.

We have suggested that the federal government should be prepared to pay about half of the total monetary outlays for higher education that are paid from public sources in the course of forwarding these endeavors.

INSTITUTIONS OF HIGHER EDUCATION

Higher education, state and federal support notwithstanding, should take the major initiative in determining its own future. Too often it has been the recipient of change rather than the originator of it. A new generation of leadership is required if higher education is to design its future and not merely live within the framework that others will have built for it. Heavy responsibilities thus lie with presidents and trustees, and with faculty and student leaders. We have made many suggestions for action to *institutions of higher education.* They should:

A new generation of leadership is required if higher education is to design its future and not merely live within the framework that others will have built for it.

■ Give aggressive leadership to the achievement of equality of opportunity through higher education—seeking out talent wherever it may be found, providing remedial work to overcome past deficiencies where necessary, caring for the cultural interests of new groups of students; enlarge the pool of women and members of minority groups for faculty appointments, and give special consideration to the talents of women and members of minority groups in adding to the overall excellence of the performance of higher education.

■ Search constantly for the means to improve the educational experience of students—through more choice among more diverse options, a renovated program of general education, a more constructive environment for developmental growth, more opportunities to mix work and service, among many other proposals. They should be more concerned with better teaching, with more effective curricula, and with all the other dimensions of academic quality—seeking more optimal modes of curricular organization and instructional presentation.

■ Make better use of resources—particularly by seeking ways to achieve an improvement in quality while holding the increasing cost per student to the level of the rise in per capita disposable income (the cost of living plus the general rise in productivity of 2.5 percent), and by undertaking to release funds from old projects where better use of them can be made on new projects.

■ Solve the whole range of governance problems—problems concerned with a greater sense of purpose, more assured institutional independence, adaptation to the new situations relating to student power, faculty tenure, and collective bargaining, and structuring consultation and authority to achieve the best quality of decisions.

Higher education above all needs active leadership pressing for better ways of doing things and greater achievements. Trustees now should search more for "initiative" leaders. Faculty members must be prepared to debate about fundamental purposes and to give more attention to matters of educational policy, to the renovation of general education, to the maintenance of academic standards, to the processes of academic change, to methods of counseling and advising students, to ways of soliciting student advice about academic matters, to self-restraint in the use of the campus as a weapon in the political arena, to the wisdom of undertaking collective bargaining in individual situations, to the rules governing tenure, to the search for colleagues among women and members of minority groups, to curricular relations with the high schools, to the possibilities of greater use of the associate in arts and doctor of arts degrees, to the rewards for good teaching, to a whole range of issues often neglected over the past decade while attention was directed more toward accommodating the great influx of students, adapting to student dissent, enlarging the role of research. More faculty members are now more oriented toward their home campuses as possibilities of intercampus mobility have been reduced, and this creates the opportunity for more concern by them in the adademic welfare of their home campuses, in addition to the continuing concern of faculty members in their own individual advancement and the progress of their fields of specialization.

Faculty members must be prepared to debate about fundamental purposes, to give more attention to matters of educational policy.

PARENTS, STUDENTS, AND EMPLOYERS

Parents can assist by:

■ Not pressing too hard for attendance of their children in college right after high school

■ Being sympathetic to explorations of alternatives to college by young persons reluctant to attend college

■ Being prepared to pay rising tuitions as part of their planning of future family accounts

Students should give consideration to:

■ Getting a broad general education

■ Developing vocational skills of wide applicability

■ Exploring lifetime nonvocational interests

■ Assessing their options carefully, including "stop-outs" and three-year A.B. degree possibilities

■ Obtaining work and service experience along with academic training

■ Securing vocational guidance early in their academic careers, and developing realistic job expectations

Employers should be prepared to:

■ Assess the total academic and career record of applicants rather than relying on receipt of a degree as the one necessary and sufficient credential

RECOMMENDATIONS DESERVING SPECIAL ATTENTION

Of all of our many specific recommendations, we call particular attention to these suggestions:

Of all of our many specific recommendations,[1] we call particular attention to these suggestions:

■ Clarification of purposes, and re-creation of a great new sense of purpose

■ Reaffirmation by faculty members of their responsibility for providing inspiring teaching

■ Adoption of codes of conduct for members of the campus community that reflect the high purposes of the academic endeavor, particularly a Bill of Rights and Responsibilities

■ Development of guidelines for the exercise of public authority that will guarantee the essential independence of institutions of higher education

■ Extension and improvement of the federal Basic Opportunity Grants program

■ Creation of a better national student loan system

---

[1] For a full set of our recommendations and a collation of them by sources of action, see *A Digest of Reports and Recommendations of the Carnegie Commission on Higher Education,* forthcoming.

- Provision by the states of a sufficiency of open-access places within each state and each metropolitan area

- Provision of state financial support for private colleges and universities

- More attention at all levels to the most effective use of resources

- Introduction of variable time options for students, especially a three-year degree program for the A.B. degree

- Renovation of general education, particularly in the direction of opportunities for broad learning experiences

- Extension and improvement of a series of educational channels for young persons to enter adult life and work and service, and not through college attendance alone

- Greater participation of students in the decision-making process

- A renaissance of progressive leadership directed toward constructive change

Survival, with memories of past glories, is not enough of a program for higher education as it approaches the year 2000.

These are among the many actions that can be taken. Survival, with memories of past glories, is not enough of a program for higher education as it approaches the year 2000. Nor is it enough for society as it relies more and more in creating its future on the high skills and careful thought that higher education can so effectively supply.

A SUMMING UP

We have studied and considered the condition of higher education in the United States intensively for six years.

We find higher education in the process of recovering from a period of depression that followed a prior time of very high achievement.

We believe that higher education will continue to recover from the effects of the several crises that have recently affected it.

We have recommended a number of actions which will assist this recovery and which will aid higher education to reach new levels of achievement.

We are convinced that attaining these new levels of achievement is essential to the welfare of American society.

REFERENCES

Ashby, Eric: "The Future of the Nineteenth Century Idea of a University," *Minerva,* vol. 6, Autumn 1967.

Ashby, Eric: *Any Person, Any Study,* McGraw-Hill Book Company, New York, 1971.

Blumberg, Mark S.: *Trends and Projections of Physicians in The United States, 1967–2002,* Carnegie Commission on Higher Education, Berkeley, Calif., 1971.

Cheit, Earl F.: *The New Depression in Higher Education,* McGraw-Hill Book Company, New York, 1971.

Cheit, Earl F.: *The New Depression in Higher Education— Two Years Later,* Carnegie Commission on Higher Education, Berkeley, Calif., 1973.

Comber, L. C., and John P. Keeves: *Science Education in Nineteen Countries,* Almquist and Wiksell, Stockholm, 1973.

Eulau, Heinz, and Harold Quinley: *State Officials and Higher Education, A Survey of the Opinions and Expectations of Policy Makers in Nine States,* McGraw-Hill Book Company, New York, 1970.

Gross, Edward, and Paul V. Grambsch: *University Goals and Academic Power: 1964–1971,* forthcoming, November 1973, McGraw-Hill Book Company, New York.

Halsey, A. H.: in *The Times Higher Education Supplement, London Times,* May 25, 1973.

Hechinger, Fred M.: "Pupil Performance: Home Is A Crucial Factor," *New York Times,* May 27, 1973.

Hodgkinson, Harold L.: *Institutions in Transition: A Profile of Change in Higher Education,* McGraw-Hill Book Company, New York, 1971.

Hutchins, Robert M.: *The Learning Society,* Praeger, New York, 1968.

Juster, Thomas F. (ed.): *Education, Income and Human Behavior,* McGraw-Hill Book Company, New York, forthcoming.

Lee, Gordon C., (ed.): *Crusade Against Ignorance: Thomas Jefferson and Education,* Classics in Education #6, Teachers College Press, Columbia University, New York, 1961.

Machlup, Fritz: *The Production and Distribution of Knowledge in the United States,* Princeton University Press, Princeton, 1962.

Mayhew, Lewis B.: *Graduate and Professional Education, 1980, A Survey of Institutional Plans,* McGraw-Hill Book Company, New York, 1970.

O'Neill, June: *Resource Use in Higher Education: Trends in Output and Input of American Colleges and Universities, 1930–1967,* Carnegie Commission on Higher Education, Berkeley, Calif., 1971.

O'Neill, June: *Sources of Funds to Colleges and Universities,* Carnegie Commission on Higher Education, Berkeley, Calif., 1973.

Parsons, Talcott: *The System of Modern Societies,* Prentice Hall, Englewood Cliff, N.J., 1971.

Peterson, Richard E., and John A. Bilorusky: *May 1970: The Campus Aftermath of Camboida and Kent State,* Carnegie Commission on Higher Education, Berkeley, Calif., 1971.

Spaeth, Joe L., and Andrew M. Greeley: *Recent Alumni and Higher Education: A Survey of College Graduates,* McGraw-Hill Book Company, New York, 1970.

Taubman, Paul, and Terrence Wales: *Mental Ability and Higher Education Attainment in the 20th Century,* Carnegie Commission on Higher Education, Berkeley, Calif., 1972.

Thompson, Dennis F.: "Democracy and the Governing of the University," *The Annals of the American Academy of Political and Social Science,* vol. 404, November 1972.

Trilling, Lionel: *Mind in the Modern World,* Viking Press, New York, 1972.

Van Alstyne, William W.: "The Specific Theory of Academic Freedom and the General Issue of Civil Liberties," *The Annals of the American Academy of Political and Social Science,* vol. 404, November 1972.

Withey, Stephen B.: *A Degree and What Else? Correlates and Consequences of a College Education,* McGraw-Hill Book Company, New York, 1971.

Young, Anne M.: "The High School Class of 1972. More at Work, Fewer in College," *Monthly Labor Review,* vol. 96, June 1973, pp. 26–32.

ALTERNATIVE ENROLLMENT PROJECTIONS

TECHNICAL NOTE

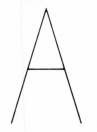

A

In *New Students and New Places,* issued in 1971, the Carnegie Commission published enrollment projections to the year 2000. At that time, the most recent enrollment data available were for fall 1970. In the years since 1970, there have been some rather unusual patterns of enrollment changes, deviating by considerable margins from the changes that would have been predicted on the basis of past trends.

Deviations from past trends have not been confined to enrollment in higher education. The rate of graduation from high school has tended to level off in the last few years for young people of both sexes (U.S. Office of Education, 1972*b,* pp. 33, 42, and 158). In addition, the birthrate has fallen sharply. The U.S. Bureau of the Census has developed two new series of population projections—Series E and Series F—that reflect these recent changes in the birthrate. In our earlier enrollment projections, we used Series D, which indicated a more rapid increase in the population in the future than do either Series E or Series F. The impact of recent changes in the birthrate, of course, does not affect our projections until about 1989 or 1990, when young people born, say, in 1972, would reach the typical age of entrance into college (17 or 18). Comparisons between Series D and Series E and F are included in Table A-1.

Because of the unusual changes that have occurred in the last few years, we have developed an alternative projection that makes use of data available in the summer of 1973. We have called it Projection II to distinguish it from the earlier Projection I.[1] We are not necessarily convinced that Projection II is more reliable than the earlier projections, but it does reflect changes that have occurred in the last few years. If these recent shifts continue as future trends, our new projections will surely prove to be more reliable. Of course, recent shifts may be purely temporary.

Before discussing the alternative projection, we need briefly to review the recent shifts in enrollment rates and other relevant data:

1   As indicated earlier, high school graduation rates have tended to level off.

[1] In *New Students and New Places,* this projection was the third and lowest of three alternatives, referred to in that document as Projections A, B, and C (Carnegie Commission, 1971).

TABLE A-1   Birthrate and number of live births, United States, actual, 1910, by race, and sex, October 1967, 1969, and 1972.

| | | | | | | | PROJECTIONS | |
YEAR	BIRTH-RATE*	LIVE BIRTHS (IN THOU-SANDS)	YEAR	BIRTH-RATE	LIVE BIRTHS (IN THOU-SANDS)	YEAR	BIRTH-RATE	LIVE BIRTHS (IN THOU-SANDS)
1910	30.1	2,777	1951	24.9	3,823		SERIES D	
1920	27.7	2,950	1952	25.1	3,913			
1930	21.3	2,618	1953	25.0	3,965	1972–73	17.1	3,581
1931	20.2	2,506	1954	25.3	4,078	1977–78	19.9	4,416
1932	19.5	2,440	1955	25.0	4,104	1982–83	20.9	4,949
1933	18.4	2,307	1956	25.2	4,218	1987–88	19.7	4,945
1934	19.0	2,396	1957	25.3	4,308	1992–93	18.0	4,788
1935	18.7	2,377	1958	24.5	4,255		SERIES E	
1936	18.4	2,355	1959	24.0	4,245			
1937	18.7	2,413	1960	23.7	4,258	1972–73	15.5	3,242
1938	19.2	2,496	1961	23.3	4,268	1977–78	17.2	3,773
1939	18.8	2,466	1962	22.4	4,167	1982–83	18.2	4,190
1940	19.4	2,559	1963	21.7	4,098	1987–88	17.3	4,165
1941	20.3	2,703	1964	21.0	4,027	1992–93	15.7	3,948
1942	22.2	2,989	1965	19.4	3,760		SERIES F	
1943	22.7	3,104	1966	18.4	3,606			
1944	21.2	2,939	1967	17.8	3,521	1972–73	14.8	3,112
1945	20.4	2,858	1968	17.5	3,502	1977–78	15.7	3,417
1946	24.1	3,411	1969	17.7	3,571	1982–83	16.2	3,674
1947	26.6	3,817	1970	18.2	3,725	1987–88	15.3	3,598
1948	24.9	3,637	1971	17.2	3,554	1992–93	13.9	3,365
1949	24.5	3,649	1972	15.6	3,256			
1950	24.1	3,632						

* Live births per 1,000 population.
SOURCES: U.S. Bureau of the Census (1960; 1965; 1972a, pp. 11–12, 1972b, p. 50).

2   According to data collected annually by the U.S. Bureau of the Census in its *Current Population Survey,* the percentage of college-age white men enrolled in institutions of higher education, which had been rising rapidly throughout the 1960s, reached a peak in 1969 and then fell sharply (Table A-2). Only a portion of this change is attributable to the purely statistical effects of changes in military procurement.[2] Among white women aged 18 to 19, the enrollment rate tended to level off

[2] Since census data refer only to the noninstitutional civilian population, a sharp buildup in military force would, by itself, result in a rise in the college enrollment *rate,* if accessions to active duty came disproportionately from the population that would not otherwise attend college.

TABLE A-2   Percentage of persons aged 14 to 34 enrolled in college by age, race, and sex, October 1967, 1969, and 1972

| | PERCENTAGE ENROLLED | | | | | |
| | MEN | | | WOMEN | | |
RACE AND AGE	1967	1969	1972	1967	1969	1972
WHITE						
TOTAL, 14 to 34 YEARS	15.0	16.4	15.2	9.0	9.7	10.2
14 TO 17	1.4	1.6	1.7	2.2	1.7	2.0
18 TO 19	43.7	47.3	39.6	33.7	35.8	35.6
20 TO 21	45.5	47.3	37.5	23.7	24.6	26.8
22 TO 24	21.1	23.5	21.0	6.7	9.1	8.7
25 TO 29	9.9	11.7	12.4	2.8	3.7	5.0
30 TO 34	4.8	5.4	5.7	2.3	3.0	2.9
BLACK						
TOTAL, 14 TO 34 YEARS	6.7	7.3	10.4	4.9	6.8	8.1
14 TO 17	0.8	1.0	1.7	1.0	0.9	1.3
18 TO 19	21.8	21.7	23.0	14.8	24.3	24.7
20 TO 21	19.6	24.8	24.0	13.4	17.4	16.4
22 TO 24	8.3	9.2	17.1	4.1	4.5	7.8
25 TO 29	2.7	2.4	7.3	3.9	3.4	4.6
30 TO 34	2.2	1.9	5.2	0.7	2.6	5.2

SOURCES: U.S. Bureau of the Census (1970, pp. 8–9, and tables for 1972 provided in advance of publication).

after 1969, whereas among women aged 20 to 21, the rate continued to rise.

In contrast, enrollment rates of young black men and women continued to rise between 1969 and 1972. This was true for all age groups, except those aged 20 to 21. Enrollment rates of black men, however, rose more rapidly than those of black women.

3   Non-degree-credit enrollment has been rising very rapidly in recent years. Of the major categories of enrollment shown in Chart A-1, non-degree-credit, or "occupational" enrollment in two-year colleges, is the only category that increased in 1971 and 1972 more rapidly than the Commission's Projection I had indicated. Prebaccalaureate degree-credit enrollment in four-year institutions actually declined in 1971 and 1972.

4   Graduate resident enrollment (all graduate enrollment except in extension programs) also increased much less rapidly than our Projection I had indicated. Surveys conducted by the Council of Graduate Schools showed increases of only about 2 percent from 1970 to 1971, and again from 1971 to 1972. These increases were much smaller than those that had prevailed in

CHART A-1   Enrollment in higher education—total, prebaccalaureate degree-credit in two-year and four-year institutions, and non-degree-credit in two-year institutions—actual, 1959, or 1960 to 1972, and projections based on past trends, 1971 and 1972 (in thousands)

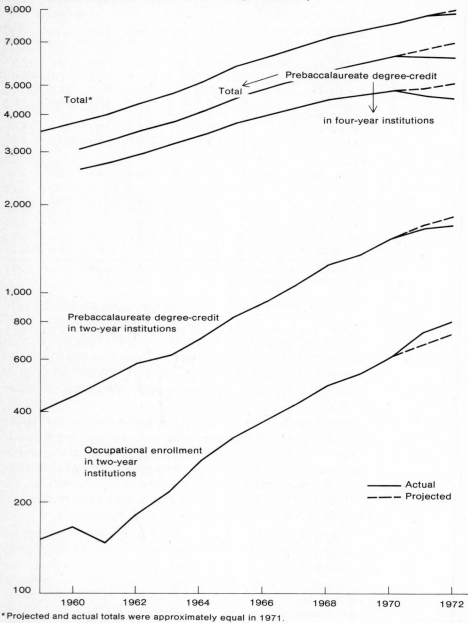

*Projected and actual totals were approximately equal in 1971.

SOURCE: U.S. Office of Education data, adjusted by Carnegie Commission staff; projections by Carnegie Commission staff.

the late 1960s. U.S. Office of Education data, which have been made available to us in advance of publication, show a slight decline in graduate resident enrollment between 1970 and 1971. Statistics on graduate enrollment in 1972 are not yet available. However, most of the available evidence indicates that the sluggish behavior of graduate enrollment in the last few years is primarily attributable to cutbacks in fellowship programs and in graduate admissions in leading graduate schools that had formerly enrolled large numbers of fellowship holders.

For example, the Carnegie Commission's fall 1971 enrollment survey (Peterson, 1972) showed that applications for entry into graduate schools increased more sharply than admissions between 1970 and 1971.[3] Both the Commission's survey and the survey of the Council of Graduate Schools showed that very little of the modest increase in first-time enrollment went to universities—most of it went to other four-year institutions (chiefly state colleges). As further evidence that the "demand" for graduate education continues to be very strong, a number of leading graduate schools have recently reported that applications for admission in the fall of 1973 are up sharply.[4]

5   In contrast with graduate enrollment, first-professional degree enrollment has been rising rapidly. Between 1970 and 1971, first-professional degree enrollment increased about 11 percent, according to unpublished OE data. Complete statistics on first-professional degree enrollment are not yet available for 1972, but, in the two most important groups of schools offering first-professional degrees—law schools and medical schools—the behavior of enrollment in 1972 was quite different. First-time medical school enrollment increased about 10 percent ("Women Students . . . ," 1973), but first-time law school enrollment was down about 3 percent, in contrast with the rapidly rising enrollment in the previous several years. The American Bar Association attributed the decline to admission cutbacks that were forced on the schools as a result of movement into the upper classes of the two large entrant classes of the preceding two years (Carnegie Commission, 1973a, p. 102).

[3] See the more extensive discussion in Carnegie Commission on Higher Education, *College Graduates and Jobs* (1973a, Sec. 8).

[4] See "Graduate-School Applications Rise" (Semas, 1973). This same article, however, indicates that applications for some of these schools had dropped between 1971 and 1972.

To sum up, then, there is little or no evidence that the propensity for college graduates to seek more advanced education has generally declined. There is, however, evidence that the upward trend in high school graduation rates has leveled off, perhaps temporarily, and that the proportion of high school graduates immediately going on to college has declined somewhat from a peak in the late 1960s. Moreover, the decline has occurred primarily among white men.

These shifts in the trends of high school graduation and college entrance rates mean that the number of recipients of bachelor's degrees is not likely to rise as rapidly in the mid-1970s as our earlier projections suggested, and thus there will be fewer potential entrants to graduate and professional schools. If the changes that have characterized the last few years continue, this is likely to be true beyond the mid-1970s.

In developing Projection II (Table A-3), we have made the following changes as compared with Projection I:

1   Adjusted downward slightly both high school graduation rates and college entrance rates

2   Assumed that the proportion of bachelor's recipients (the average of the most recent four years) going on to postbaccalaureate training would remain constant at about the 1969 level

3   Used Census Bureau Series E in connection with projections for 1990 and 2000

TABLE A-3   Opening fall enrollment in higher education, by level, actual 1970, and projected 1980 to 2000 (numbers in thousands)

	1970	1980	1990	2000	PERCENTAGE CHANGE		
					1970– 1980	1980– 1990	1990– 2000
PROJECTION I—PREPARED IN 1971*							
TOTAL ENROLLMENT	8,649	13,015	12,654	16,559	50.5	—2.8	30.9
PREBACCALAUREATE	7,443	11,082	10,587	14,123	48.9	—4.5	33.4
POSTBACCALAUREATE	1,206	1,933	2,068	2,436	60.3	7.0	17.8
PROJECTION II—PREPARED IN 1973†							
TOTAL ENROLLMENT	8,649	11,446	10,555	13,209	33.3	—7.8	25.1
PREBACCALAUREATE	7,443	9,720	8,882	11,221	30.6	—8.6	26.3
POSTBACCALAUREATE	1,206	1,726	1,673	1,988	43.1	—3.1	18.8

* See Carnegie Commission on Higher Education, *New Students and New Places* (1971). Referred to in that report as "Projection C"

† Carnegie Commission staff, 1973

Other assumptions, such as the one that non-degree-credit enrollment would account for 18 percent of the male and 16 percent of the female increase in prebaccalaureate enrollments, have been maintained.

Enrollment changes for the nation tell us nothing about the considerable underlying variation by state (see Table A-4). For the country as a whole, opening fall enrollments rose by 8 percent between 1970 and 1972, but in several states the rate of growth was more than double the overall average: Nevada and South Carolina (33 percent); Delaware (19 percent); and Vermont, Virginia, and Wyoming (18 percent). Other states—Minnesota, Montana, Nebraska, New Hampshire, North Dakota, and South Dakota—appear to have lost students, although the preliminary nature of the 1972 data implies that late reporting might account for some apparent declines.

The pattern of enrollment changes by states defies simple explanation. There is little relationship between changes in population and college enrollment. This suggests that such factors as changes in tuition charges and in acceptance of out-of-state applications, among others, are probably important.

We now add Projection III. This takes into account the implications of future trends and the recommendations in our recent report, *Toward A Learning Society* (1973b). We expect (and recommend) in that report that enrollments of "nontraditional" students will expand at a faster rate in the future for the reasons given therein. We define *nontraditional* students, for purposes of statistical presentation, as part-time degree-credit students and non-degree-credit students whether part-time or full-time; with full-time degree-credit students defined as *traditional*.

TABLE A-4   Changes in total enrollment in higher education by state, 1970 to 1972 (numbers in thousands)

STATE	1970	1972	PERCENTAGE CHANGE
ALABAMA	102.7	118.5	15.4
ALASKA	10.1	11.7	15.8
ARIZONA	110.1	123.7	12.4
ARKANSAS	51.6	53.9	4.5
CALIFORNIA	1,255.8	1,310.7	4.4
COLORADO	121.6	127.9	5.2
CONNECTICUT	124.9	130.9	4.8
DELAWARE	23.9	28.5	19.3
DISTRICT OF COLUMBIA	75.9	80.5	6.1

TABLE A-4   continued

STATE	1970	1972	PERCENTAGE CHANGE
FLORIDA	234.2	255.4	9.1
GEORGIA	126.2	140.8	11.6
HAWAII	36.5	42.4	16.2
IDAHO	34.6	34.5	—0.3
ILLINOIS	453.6	483.5	6.6
INDIANA	191.2	201.4	2.7
IOWA	108.4	109.5	1.0
KANSAS	101.3	108.0	6.6
KENTUCKY	96.9	108.1	11.6
LOUISIANA	120.8	134.6	11.4
MAINE	32.2	34.6	7.5
MARYLAND	148.6	167.7	12.9
MASSACHUSETTS	303.0	319.9	5.6
MICHIGAN	394.1	407.4	3.4
MINNESOTA	159.1	148.3	—7.3
MISSISSIPPI	73.1	80.3	9.9
MISSOURI	183.6	188.9	2.9
MONTANA	29.7	28.0	—6.1
NEBRASKA	66.4	66.0	—0.6
NEVADA	13.0	17.3	33.1
NEW HAMPSHIRE	29.0	28.3	—2.5
NEW JERSEY	210.4	241.2	14.6
NEW MEXICO	43.7	48.0	9.8
NEW YORK	776.6	842.3	8.5
NORTH CAROLINA	171.5	193.4	12.8
NORTH DAKOTA	30.5	29.8	—2.4
OHIO	371.4	385.6	3.8
OKLAHOMA	109.6	121.9	11.2
OREGON	114.3	123.3	7.9
PENNSYLVANIA	410.5	429.8	4.7
RHODE ISLAND	45.1	49.4	9.5
SOUTH CAROLINA	70.3	93.8	33.4
SOUTH DAKOTA	30.8	29.0	—6.2
TENNESSEE	135.5	147.3	8.7
TEXAS	438.6	458.7	4.6
UTAH	79.1	81.7	3.3
VERMONT	22.1	26.0	17.7
VIRGINIA	149.2	176.0	18.0
WASHINGTON	180.4	194.3	7.7
WEST VIRGINIA	63.3	64.7	2.2
WISCONSIN	201.6	217.1	7.7
WYOMING	15.0	17.7	18.0
TOTAL*	8,498.1	9,166.6	7.9

* Includes outlying areas and service schools.

SOURCE: U.S. Office of Education (1972a); and prepublication release, preliminary data, December 1972.

TABLE A-5 Opening fall enrollment in higher education, actual 1970, and projected 1980 to 2000

	PROJECTION I*				PROJECTION II*				PROJECTION III†			
YEAR	NUMBER OF PERSONS	PERCENT-AGE CHANGE	FTE	PERCENT-AGE CHANGE	NUMBER OF PERSONS	PERCENT-AGE CHANGE	FTE	PERCENT-AGE CHANGE	NUMBER OF PERSONS	PERCENT-AGE CHANGE	FTE	PERCENT-AGE CHANGE
1970	8,649		6,964		8,649		6,764		8,649		6,764	
1980	13,015	50.5	9,971	47.4	11,446	33.3	8,770	29.7	11,670	34.9	8,896	31.5
1990	12,654	−2.8	9,621	−3.5	10,555	−7.8	8,026	−8.5	11,402	−2.3	8,502	−4.4
2000	16,559	30.9	12,475	29.7	13,209	25.1	9,951	24.0	14,295	25.4	10,561	24.2

* See notes, Table A-3

†Estimates by Carnegie Commission staff based on Projection II and adjusted to reflect alternative trend assumptions and recommendations in *Toward a Learning Society* (Carnegie Commission, 1973b).

Some of these nontraditional students will not appear in statistics on opening fall enrollments. This is especially true of many part-time non-degree-credit students served in short-term extension programs.

Limiting our attention, then, to only those students enrolled at the opening of classes in the fall, Projection III adds 5 percent to the projections of nontraditional students in 1980 as compared with those estimated in Projection II, and 20 percent in 1990 and 2000. This adds about 225,000 students to headcount enrollments in 1980, and 125,000 on an FTE basis; 850,000 and 475,000, respectively, in 1990; and *1,085,000* and *610,000* in 2000 (see Table A-5).

We suggest a modest increase in the 1970s, first, because enrollment patterns for four of the years in the 1970s are already determined, and, second, because it will take time for attitudes and policies to change. We suggest a much more substantial increase in the 1980s, particularly because colleges and universities will be actively searching for nontraditional students to offset the decline in traditional students.

Projection III wipes out almost half of the difference (on a headcount basis) in 1990 between Projection I and Projection II, but less than this on an FTE basis.

Projection III is based upon expected *net* increases in enrollments over Projection II. (1) Net increases will be less than gross increases in nontraditional students because some of the increase in nontraditional students will be at the expense of enrollments of traditional students to the extent that part-time and non-degree-credit enrollments are made more attractive; and (2) the suggestions in *Toward a Learning Society* are also aimed at making further education more attractive as compared with higher education and this will tend to draw both traditional and nontraditional students out of higher education into further education.

Projection III, in any event, is based upon little in the way of hard facts and actual experience. It is indicative of only one among a large number of possibilities.

Projected current expenditures of higher education in 1980 would run about $600 million higher as a result of Projection III as compared with Projection II.

The types of institutions most likely to gain from a shift toward more nontraditional students are the community colleges and, to a lesser extent, the comprehensive colleges and universities.

REFERENCES

Carnegie Commission on Higher Education: *New Students and New Places: Policies for the Future Growth and Development of American Higher Education,* McGraw-Hill Book Company, New York, 1971.

Carnegie Commission on Higher Education: *College Graduates and Jobs: Adjusting to a New Labor Market Situation,* McGraw-Hill Book Company, New York, 1973a.

Carnegie Commission on Higher Education: *Toward a Learning Society: Alternative Channels to Life, Work, and Service,* McGraw-Hill Book Company, New York, 1973b.

Peterson, Richard E.: *American College and University Enrollment Trends in 1971,* Carnegie Commission on Higher Education, Berkeley, Calif., 1972.

Semas, P. W.: "Graduate-School Applications Rise," *Chronicle of Higher Education,* Mar. 5, 1973.

U.S. Bureau of the Census: *Historical Statistics of the United States: Colonial Times to 1957,* ser. B-6 and B-19, Washington, D.C., 1960

U.S. Bureau of the Census: *Historical Statistics of the United States: Continuation to 1962 and Revisions,* ser. B-6 and B-19, Washington, D.C., 1965.

U.S. Bureau of the Census: "School Enrollment: October 1969," *Current Population Reports,* ser. P-20, no. 206, Washington, D.C., 1970.

U.S. Bureau of the Census: "Projections of the Population of the United States, by Age and Sex: 1972 to 2020," *Current Population Reports,* ser. P-25, no. 493, December 1972a.

U.S. Bureau of the Census: *Statistical Abstract of the United States,* Washington, D.C., 1972b.

U.S. Bureau of the Census: Estimates of the Population of the United States and Components of Change," *Current Population Reports,* ser. P-25, no. 499, May 1973.

U.S. Office of Education: *Digest of Educational Statistics, 1971,* Washington, D.C., 1972a.

U.S. Office of Education, National Center for Educational Statistics: *Projections of Educational Statistics to 1980–81,* Washington, D.C., 1972*b.*

"Women Students in United States Medical Schools, Past and Present Trends," *Journal of Medical Education,* vol. 48, pp. 186–189, February 1973.

PROSPECTS FOR MINORITY-GROUP AND FEMALE PARTICIPATION IN HIGHER EDUCATION FACULTIES, 1970–2000

TECHNICAL NOTE

Present efforts to increase the relative participation of women and members of minority groups in college and university faculties are long overdue. However, as the rate of increase in enrollments and demand for faculty members in higher education slows down in the 1970s, it will become increasingly difficult to raise the proportions of faculty members who are women or members of minority groups. In the 1980s, there might be a reduction in the total number of faculty members. If so, it will be even more difficult than in the 1970s to achieve affirmative action goals. In the 1990s, according to our projections, an increase in enrollments and in the demand for faculty members is likely to occur again, but not at anything resembling the rate of increase to which higher education was accustomed in the 1960s. One might well ask, then, how effective affirmative action programs can be.

That relatively few women and members of minority groups are now on the faculties of colleges and universities is apparent from Tables B-1 and B-2. Table B-1 indicates that women comprised approximately 38 percent of the civilian labor force in 1970 and participated at a substantially lower rate than did men. Minorities—defined throughout this technical note as blacks, Asians, Native Americans and persons of Spanish origin[1]—represented almost 15 percent of the labor force in 1970, but they participated at a slightly higher rate than did the majority. On the other hand, women and members of minorities represented 22.5 percent and 5.3 percent, respectively, of all full-time faculty members in colleges and universities. These levels fall far short of what one might expect when viewing the demographic characteristics of the labor force. The reasons for these relatively small numbers are quite complex and are beyond the scope of this note. They have, however, been discussed in earlier Commission reports—see, for example, *Opportunities for Women in Higher Education.*

This note will examine the need for new faculty members to the year 2000, and discuss the possibilities for raising the levels of participation of women and members of minorities on col-

NOTE: This technical report was prepared by John A. Ferguson of the staff of the Carnegie Commission.

[1] As defined in "Persons of Spanish Origin in the United States: March 1972 and 1971" (U.S. Bureau of the Census, 1973, p. 1): "Includes persons who identified themselves as being of Mexican, Puerto Rican, Cuban, Central or South American, or other Spanish origin."

TABLE B-1   Women and members of minorities in the civilian labor force, 1970

	PERCENTAGE OF TOTAL	PARTICIPATION RATE*
MALES	61.9	79.7
FEMALES	38.1	42.6
MEMBERS OF THE MAJORITY	85.1	59.5
MEMBERS OF MINORITIES	14.9	61.3

* Percentage of the population group 16 years of age or older in the civilian labor force.

SOURCE: *Manpower Report of the President, 1972.*

TABLE B-2   Women and members of minorities on college and university faculties, 1970 (percentage distributions of weighted estimates, full-time faculty)

MALES	77.5
FEMALES	22.5
MEMBERS OF THE MAJORITY	94.7
MEMBERS OF MINORITIES	5.3

SOURCE: Carnegie Commission Survey of Faculty and Student Opinion, 1969.

lege and university faculties to more nearly reflect those in the total labor force. It should be noted at the outset that women and members of minorities constitute different fractions of the faculty in different types of institutions. For example, the percentage of women on college and university faculties ranged from 11 percent in the research universities to 27 percent in the two-year colleges; and the percentage of members of minorities ranged from about 2 percent in the two-year colleges to 10 percent in the liberal arts colleges.[2]

THE NEED FOR NEW FACULTY

In an earlier note (Technical Note A), enrollment trends to the year 2000 were discussed. Because the total number of faculty members depends on the number of students pursuing postsecondary education, it is possible to speculate on how the

[2] These percentages are derived from the Carnegie Commission Survey of Faculty and Student Opinion. The classifications of institutions are described in *New Students and New Places* (Carnegie Commission on Higher Education, 1971, Appendix A).

total number of faculty members will change during the years 1970 to 2000 (Chart B-1). These projections of full-time faculty members are based on the assumption that an overall incremental student-faculty ratio of 20 to 1 will apply throughout the period.[3] Such an incremental ratio would slightly raise the total student-faculty ratio from its 1970 figure of approximately 18 to 1, and this seems quite probable for at least three reasons. First, in many areas of the country, there are already pressures to increase the student-faculty ratio in efforts to increase productivity and accountability. Second, financial retrenchment coupled with a high proportion of tenured faculty has necessitated an increase in the student-faculty ratio in many colleges and universities. Third, a substantial part of future growth in

[3] Full-time-equivalent students and full-time faculty. Excellent discussions of the changing student-faculty ratios can be found in Cartter (forthcoming) and Balderston and Radner (1971).

CHART B-1   Projections of full-time faculty and full-time-equivalent students in U.S. colleges and universities, 1970–2000 (numbers in thousands)

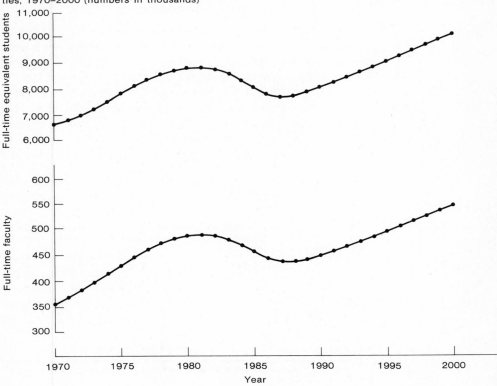

enrollments will undoubtedly be assumed by the two-year colleges, and these institutions traditionally have a much higher ratio (26 to 1) than universities (14 to 1). The assumption of a 20 to 1 ratio then leads to the projection in Chart B-1, which shows the total number of full-time faculty increasing until 1981, when it declines until about 1987. After that, it increases at a slightly slower rate than it did during the 1970s.[4]

The estimates of total full-time faculty requirements for 1970 to the year 2000 are shown in Table B-3. Since the best available evidence indicates that there is no *net* movement of senior faculty between academic and nonacademic positions, and that this situation is likely to continue, it is treated as a "wash" item for the purposes of this note (see Cartter, forthcoming). Although the percentage increase in the size of the faculty will only be a fraction of what it was in the 1960s, both the 1970s and the 1990s will produce about the same number of new hires on college and university faculties as were produced in the 1960s. This is because the size of the faculty in 1970 and in 1990 is so much larger than it was in 1960.

These new hires are only partially accounted for by changes in enrollment. Annual retirement and mortality rates—as a percentage of the total faculty—were quite low in the 1960s, and will be quite low in the 1980s, but the rapid expansion of faculty during the 1960s will cause these rates to escalate substantially in the 1990s. During the 1960s, replacement needs created by faculty attrition accounted for about 25 percent of all new hires. In the 1970s, replacements will account for 39 percent of new hires; during the 1980s, with a decline in enrollments, they will

[4]This note is based on Projection II in Technical Note A. Under the assumptions of Projection III, there would be many more faculty openings.

TABLE B-3   Full-time faculty new hires 1960–1970, and projected to 2000 (cumulative totals needed for replacement and expansion; numbers in thousands)

PERIOD	FACULTY NEW HIRES	PERCENTAGE INCREASE IN SIZE OF TOTAL FACULTY
1960–1970*	224.7	107.7
1970–1980	222.7	38.6
1980–1990	47.1	—8.5
1990–2000	238.0	22.4
1970–2000	507.8	55.2

* Figures to 1970 are derived from U.S. Office of Education data. Figures after 1970 are estimated.

represent almost 100 percent of new hires; and in the 1990s, as the "1960s" faculty ages, they will account for 57 percent of new hires. Thus, the number of new hires will depend, in large measure, on faculty attrition.

Table B-4 analyzes faculty requirements by introducing two more dimensions. First, faculty needs will be quite different for two-year colleges than for other institutions of higher education. In *New Students and New Places,* the Carnegie Commission (1971, pp. 136–137) estimated that the percentage of students enrolled in two-year colleges would gradually increase to about one-third of total enrollments by the year 2000. Thus an increasingly large proportion of new faculty will be employed by these institutions in the years ahead. Second, the needs for faculty possessing a doctorate will be quite different from the needs for faculty possessing a master's or other appropriate degree. Cartter (forthcoming) has examined the implications of various assumptions about the market for Ph.D.'s, and the best available evidence suggests that about one-quarter of new faculty in two-year colleges, and about three-quarters of new faculty in four-year colleges and universities, will possess a doctorate. Applying these estimates of degree requirements and institutional needs to the total number of new faculty members required produces the distribution shown in Table B-4. Although the four-year colleges and universities will need many more doctorate holders than will the two-year colleges, the needs for master's degree holders are more evenly distributed between the two categories of institutions. This is important because it is also among the master's degree holders that opportunities to recruit women and members of minorities will be greatest in the immediate future.

TABLE B-4   Full-time faculty new hires by type of institution and degree, 1970–2000 (5-year cumulative totals; numbers in thousands)

	2-YEAR COLLEGES			4-YEAR COLLEGES & UNIVERSITIES		
	DOC-TORATE	MASTER'S & OTHERS	TOTAL	DOC-TORATE	MASTER'S & OTHERS	TOTAL
1970–1975	7.8	23.2	31.0	64.2	21.4	85.6
1975–1980	8.1	24.1	32.2	55.4	18.5	73.9
1980–1985	0.7	2.2	2.9	15.4	5.1	20.5
1985–1990	1.7	5.2	6.9	12.6	4.2	16.8
1990–1995	9.8	29.4	39.2	55.1	18.3	73.4
1995–2000	10.6	31.6	42.2	62.4	20.8	83.2
1970–2000	38.7	115.7	154.4	265.1	88.3	353.4

THE GRADUATE POOL

No affirmative action program can succeed in raising the participation rates of women and members of minorities on college faculties unless a supply of qualified persons is available. Traditionally, such a supply was found in the graduate schools. Notable exceptions included the absorption of high school teachers into the faculties of new two-year colleges. However, during the next three decades it is reasonable to expect that the vast majority of new faculty members will probably be recruited from the graduate pool. It is useful, therefore, to examine the nature of that pool.

The distribution of women and members of minorities among college graduates is striking. Women accounted for almost 47 percent and members of minorities for almost 9 percent of persons with exactly four years of college, according to the U.S. Bureau of the Census in 1972 (Table B-5). But while the percentage of women declined to less than 31 percent of those who had completed five or more years of college, the percentage of minority-group members rose to almost 10 percent of the same group. It would appear that members of minorities exhibit a greater tendency to pursue graduate education once in college than do women and the majority, but further research is required to fully support such an assertion.

In 1969, the Carnegie Commission Survey of Faculty and Student Opinion included a detailed survey of graduate students. Based on that survey, Table B-6 shows the distribution of graduate students by type of degree sought. "Doctorate" is taken to represent any doctoral degree, and "Master's" represents any master's degree excluding professional degrees. Proportionately more male majorities pursued the doctorate than other

TABLE B-5   Highest level of education attained by women and members of minorities in the United States, March 1972 (numbers in thousands)*

	4 YEARS OF COLLEGE COMPLETED		5 YEARS OR MORE OF COLLEGE COMPLETED	
	NUMBER	PERCENTAGE	NUMBER	PERCENTAGE
MALE	5,089	53.3	3,918	69.5
FEMALE	4,460	46.7	1,723	30.5
MEMBERS OF THE MAJORITY	8,741	91.5	5,091	90.2
MEMBERS OF MINORITIES	808	8.5	550	9.8
TOTAL	9,549	100.0	5,641	100.0

* Refers to population 21 years of age and older.
SOURCE: U.S. Bureau of the Census (1972).

TABLE B-6   Women and members of minorities in graduate school: degree pursued (percentage distributions of weighted estimates)

	MEMBERS OF THE MAJORITY		MEMBERS OF MINORITIES		
	MALE	FEMALE	MALE	FEMALE	TOTAL
DOCTORATE	74.3	16.7	7.5	1.5	100.0
MASTER'S	61.1	31.6	4.8	2.5	100.0
OTHER	62.2	29.5	5.2	3.1	100.0
TOTAL	65.9	26.8	5.3	2.0	100.0

SOURCE: Carnegie Commission Survey of Faculty and Student Opinion, 1969.

degrees, and an unusually low proportion of women pursued the doctorate. But there are also proportionately more women and members of minorities in graduate schools than on the faculty (compare with Table B-2). An attempt to identify the distribution of graduate students seeking a career in higher education yielded data in Table B-7. Majority candidates for the doctorate, particularly white women, tended to expect to pursue a career in higher education more so than members of minorities. Only minor differences were exhibited among master's degree candidates, one-fifth of whom were seeking a career in higher education.

These data are further refined in Tables B-8 and B-9, which show percentage distributions of graduate students who were seeking a career in higher education. Almost half of the majority males pursuing the doctorate specialized in the humanities and physical sciences, and more than half of the master's degree candidates were in the humanities and education (Table B-8). Women tended to specialize in the humanities and education irrespective of the degree sought. The high proportion of minority males in engineering is accounted for by the unusually high percentage of Asian-Americans specializing in this area. In Table B-9, majority males far outnumber other types of graduate students in virtually every field of specialization. Shortages of women and members of minorities are particularly acute at the doctoral level. With very few exceptions, the proportions of these groups are significantly lower than the proportions they represent of total faculty (Table B-2). Thus, it would appear highly unlikely that colleges and universities—particularly the research universities which recruit heavily from the doctorate pool—could significantly increase the numbers of women and minorities on their faculties under present circumstances.

TABLE B-7 Job expectations by graduate students (percentage distributions of weighted estimates)

| | MEMBERS OF THE MAJORITY | | | | MEMBERS OF MINORITIES | | | | | | |
| | MALE | | FEMALE | | MALE | | FEMALE | | ALL | | |
	DOC-TORATE	MAS-TER'S	DOC-TORATE	MAS-TER'S	DOC-TORATE	MAS-TER'S	DOC-TORATE	MAS-TER'S	DOC-TORATE	MAS-TER'S	TOTAL*
TEACH IN A JUNIOR COLLEGE	0.7	3.4	1.6	7.2	0.4	1.9	0.0	2.7	0.8	4.5	2.9
TEACH IN A 4-YEAR INSTITUTION	41.9	13.4	52.3	11.4	31.6	8.3	28.8	10.0	42.7	12.4	17.7
RESEARCH IN A 4-YEAR INSTITUTION	4.2	0.7	2.8	0.7	7.0	2.1	6.9	8.6	4.2	0.9	1.7
HIGHER EDUCATION ADMINISTRATION	3.4	3.1	2.0	2.7	1.1	1.8	10.0	5.1	3.1	3.0	2.7
ALL OTHER JOBS	49.8	79.4	41.3	78.0	59.9	85.9	54.3	73.6	49.2	79.2	75.0
TOTAL	100.0	100.0	100.0	100.0	100.0	100.0	100.0	100.0	100.0	100.0	100.0

* Includes all other degrees.

SOURCE: Carnegie Commission Survey of Faculty and Student Opinion, 1969.

TABLE B-8   Characteristics of graduate students who plan to pursue an academic career by field of specialization (percentage distributions of weighted estimates)

| | MEMBERS OF THE MAJORITY | | | | MEMBERS OF MINORITIES | | | |
| | MALE | | FEMALE | | MALE | | FEMALE | |
	DOCTORATE	MASTER'S	DOCTORATE	MASTER'S	DOCTORATE	MASTER'S	DOCTORATE	MASTER'S
SOCIAL SCIENCES	15.2	8.6	12.9	7.3	11.9	0.0	14.5	4.0
HUMANITIES	24.9	32.5	51.9	50.6	5.4	12.0	35.0	22.0
PHYSICAL SCIENCES	21.0	6.3	7.7	6.1	14.1	27.0	6.3	0.0
BIOLOGICAL SCIENCES	8.8	8.2	9.9	2.8	14.7	17.2	14.7	6.5
EDUCATION, SOCIAL WORK	16.6	28.3	14.4	22.8	5.8	17.7	29.5	65.5
NEW PROFESSIONS*	5.2	6.4	1.8	5.9	9.3	6.3	0.0	2.0
ENGINEERING	7.7	8.8	0.2	0.0	37.5	19.8	0.0	0.0
OTHERS	0.6	0.9	1.2	4.5	1.3	0.0	0.0	0.0
TOTAL	100.0	100.0	100.0	100.0	100.0	100.0	100.0	100.0

*Includes architecture, forestry, journalism, library science, etc.

SOURCE: Carnegie Commission Survey of Faculty and Student Opinion, 1969.

TABLE B-9   Characteristics of field of specialization for graduate students who plan to pursue an academic career (percentage distributions of weighted estimates)

	DOCTORATE					MASTER'S				
	MEMBERS OF THE MAJORITY		MEMBERS OF MINORITIES			MEMBERS OF THE MAJORITY		MEMBERS OF MINORITIES		
	MALE	FEMALE	MALE	FEMALE	TOTAL	MALE	FEMALE	MALE	FEMALE	TOTAL
SOCIAL SCIENCES	77.0	17.3	4.5	1.2	100.0	67.7	31.2	0.0	1.1	100.0
HUMANITIES	62.9	34.6	1.0	1.5	100.0	52.9	45.0	0.9	1.2	100.0
PHYSICAL SCIENCES	86.9	8.3	4.4	0.4	100.0	57.8	30.9	11.3	0.0	100.0
BIOLOGICAL SCIENCES	69.0	20.5	8.6	1.9	100.0	76.4	14.3	7.2	2.1	100.0
EDUCATION, SOCIAL WORK	77.8	17.8	2.1	2.3	100.0	64.6	28.5	1.8	5.1	100.0
NEW PROFESSIONS*	81.6	7.6	10.8	0.0	100.0	64.1	32.4	2.8	0.7	100.0
ENGINEERING	73.1	0.6	26.3	0.0	100.0	90.7	0.0	9.3	0.0	100.0
OTHERS	58.6	17.4	20.5	3.5	100.0	33.6	41.1	9.2	16.1	100.0
ALL FIELDS	73.4	19.4	5.9	1.3	100.0	60.2	33.4	3.3	3.1	100.0

*See Table B-8.

SOURCE: Carnegie Commission Survey of Faculty and Student Opinion, 1969.

Taking account of the career interests of graduate students and the projections of degrees conferred (Chart B-2) makes it possible to predict the proportions of women and members of minorities in the faculty recruitment pool. This, of course, assumes that graduate student characteristics do not change over the next few decades—an unlikely prospect in view of the rapidly changing demands for educated manpower in almost all fields. Our projections from Table B-4 show that, between 1970 and 2000, there would be 2.1 doctorate holders for each faculty opening requiring the doctorate, and 9.0 master's degree holders for each faculty opening requiring the master's. Or, there would be 1.2 doctorate holders and 3.6 master's holders for each faculty opening in total. Further analysis shows that among doctorate holders there would be 1.5 majority male, 0.4 women, and 0.2 members of minorities available for each faculty opening requiring the doctorate. Among master's degree holders, there would be 5.4 majority males, 3.3 women, and 0.6 members of minorities for each faculty opening requiring the master's degree. Under these conditions it would be difficult to significantly raise the participation levels of women and minorities on college and university faculties— particularly at the doctoral level. Even if women and minorities were recruited on a priority basis, women would comprise only

CHART B-2   Projections of degrees conferred, 1970–2000 (numbers in thousands)

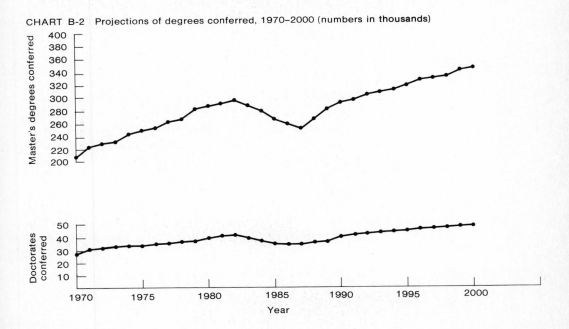

about one-third, and members of minorities about one-tenth, of the faculty in the year 2000. This situation can only be avoided through concerted efforts toward expanding the number of women and members of minorities in graduate school—particularly in those fields where they now constitute low proportions of enrolled students.

Given the length of time that most graduate students need in order to complete degree requirements, the pool for the 1970s is already reasonably well established. And with the substantially reduced need for college and university faculty in the 1980s, it will be difficult to attract able graduate students to prepare for an academic career. Nevertheless, the process of raising the levels of participation of women and members of minorities on the faculty begins in the graduate schools—both through recruiting more women and minorities and encouraging those already in graduate schools to consider a career in higher education. It is therefore imperative that the graduate schools immediately place increased emphasis on these necessary efforts.

THE AGE DISTRIBUTION OF
COLLEGE AND UNIVERSITY FACULTY

The age distribution of full-time faculty members in colleges and universities was calculated for the year 1970, and projected to the year 2000 (Table B-10). Given the slowdown in hiring during the 1970s and 1980s the percentage of younger faculty members will gradually diminish. But because the median age of faculty members for the year 1970 was relatively low, the rate of retirement will not increase noticeably until the end of the 1980s. In the 1990s, the rate of retirement will increase sharply as the "1960s" faculty ages in large numbers. These rates are depicted in Table B-11[5] along with mortality rates based on Bureau of the Census survival rates. As can be seen, total annual attrition rates decrease sharply in the 1980s but move beyond the 1970 levels in the 1990s. Retirement rates for women on faculties are substantially higher than those for men. Looking back to Table B-10, it is easy to see why. The median age for women on the faculty is actually higher than

---

[5] The rates for men are expressed as a percentage of all male faculty; for women, of all female faculty; and the total rates are expressed as a percentage of the total faculty.

TABLE B-10 Projections of full-time faculty age distributions by sex, selected years 1970–2000 (percentage distributions)

	1970			1980			1990			2000		
	MALE	FEMALE	TOTAL	MALE	FEMALE	TOTAL	MALE	FEMALE	TOTAL	MALE	FEMALE	TOTAL
30 AND UNDER	12.5	17.3	13.5	7.4	11.3	8.0	1.0	1.3	1.0	12.4	14.1	12.5
31–35	15.6	11.3	14.7	14.2	10.4	13.4	3.0	2.1	2.8	14.9	11.2	13.8
36–40	16.7	12.4	15.9	17.3	13.0	16.5	9.5	6.8	8.7	6.6	4.8	6.0
41–45	15.5	14.4	15.3	21.6	20.2	21.4	19.1	17.5	18.8	6.0	5.5	5.9
46–50	13.9	13.1	13.7	17.6	16.6	17.4	24.9	23.3	24.5	9.4	8.6	9.2
51–55	10.5	11.1	10.6	10.9	11.6	11.1	21.1	21.4	21.2	16.3	16.6	16.4
56–60	7.2	8.6	7.5	5.9	7.1	6.1	13.0	15.6	14.2	18.7	20.9	19.9
61 AND OVER	8.0	11.7	8.8	5.1	9.5	6.1	8.4	12.1	8.8	15.7	18.3	16.3

NOTE: This model assumes no changes from present practices in retirement policies, student-staff ratios, net flows to employment outside academic institutions, and the like. Cartter (1972) has discussed some of the factors that might alter these patterns.

TABLE B-11 Estimated annual attrition rates for full-time faculty, selected years 1970–2000*

	1970			1980			1990			2000		
	MALE	FEMALE	TOTAL	MALE	FEMALE	TOTAL	MALE	FEMALE	TOTAL	MALE	FEMALE	TOTAL
MORTALITY RATE	.0064	.0044	.0059	.0053	.0037	.0048	.0067	.0039	.0058	.0077	.0043	.0064
RETIREMENT RATE	.0158	.0232	.0175	.0102	.0190	.0132	.0168	.0242	.0194	.0229	.0244	.0235
TOTAL ATTRITION RATE	.0222	.0276	.0234	.0155	.0227	.0180	.0235	.0281	.0252	.0306	.0287	.0299

* See note to Table B-10.

that for men and will remain so to the turn of the century unless substantial alterations take place in hiring practices. As expected, mortality rates for women are lower than those for men. As was mentioned earlier, these models assume a zero net flow of faculty members between academic and nonacademic positions.

Since the projections of the age distributions of faculty members are based upon current personnel practices, they could well change as more women and minorities are recruited. One would expect that the median age of women, for example, would begin to drop as more young women are recruited. However, the age distributions for men are not expected to change much from the projections because fewer openings will be available during the next two decades.

THE ABSORPTION OF WOMEN AND MINORITIES

Perhaps the most difficult aspect of analyzing the ability of colleges and universities to absorb more women and minorities onto their faculties is the uncertainty concerning faculty needs for different fields of specialization. In 1969, with the exceptions of education and the new professions, the distribution of faculty members among different fields of specialization was strikingly similar in different types of institutions (Table B-12). With the recent emphasis on more vocational training for stu-

TABLE B-12   Distribution of full-time faculty members by field of specialization and type of institution (percentage distributions of weighted estimates)

	4-YEAR COLLEGES AND UNIVERSITIES	2-YEAR COLLEGES	ALL INSTI-TUTIONS†
SOCIAL SCIENCES	13.6	10.2	12.7
HUMANITIES	23.6	23.1	23.1
PHYSICAL SCIENCES	14.3	15.7	15.2
BIOLOGICAL SCIENCES	6.7	6.1	6.4
EDUCATION, SOCIAL WORK	12.6	7.1	11.1
NEW PROFESSIONS*	7.5	13.3	8.6
ENGINEERING	4.8	5.3	5.9
OTHERS	16.9	19.2	17.0
TOTAL	100.0	100.0	100.0

* See Table B-8

† Includes technical and trade schools.

SOURCE: Carnegie Commission Survey of Faculty and Student Opinion, 1969.

dents, however, it might be expected that these patterns will change during the next two decades—particularly in the two-year colleges. Trends were noted for many of these fields in the Commission's report *College Graduates and Jobs* (1973), and it would be impossible to explore all the implications of these trends in this analysis, but it is probably safe to assume that the share represented by the humanities and education will diminish as interest and demand increase in other areas— as, for example, in the health service professions.

The question about the possibilities for hiring more women and members of minorities in order to raise their participation levels to those found in the labor force as a whole depends upon the effect of different hiring patterns on the present distribution of women and minorities. Charts B-3 and B-4 apply

CHART B-3   Projections of women as a percentage of full-time faculty, 1970–2000, under various hiring rates

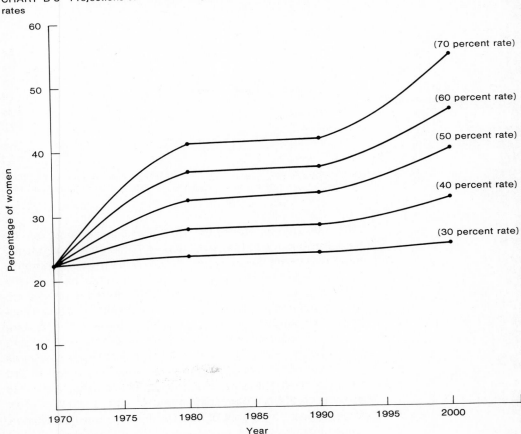

CHART B-4　Projections of minority-group members as a percentage of full-time faculty, 1970–2000, under various hiring rates

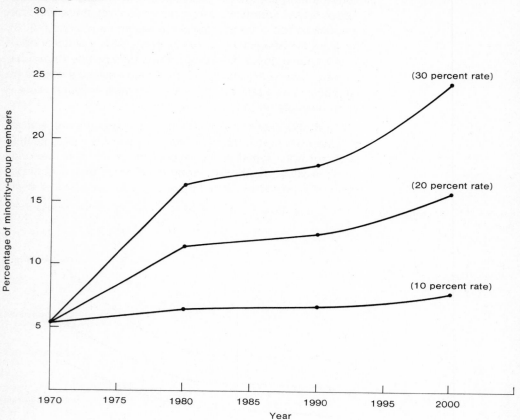

differential hiring rates to the 1970 population and project the new distributions to the year 2000. If 70 percent of all faculty hired during the period were women, women would comprise 55 percent of the faculty in 2000. On the other hand, if only 30 percent of all faculty hired during the period were women, they would comprise 26 percent of the faculty in 2000. Similarly, if 30 percent of all faculty hired during this period were members of minorities, they would amount to almost 25 percent of the faculty in 2000; while if only 10 percent of new hires were minorities, they would total less than 8 percent of the faculty in 2000. These two charts would indicate that in order to achieve, by 2000, a participation rate equal to that in the labor force, almost 50 percent of new faculty hires must be women, and almost 20 percent must be members of minorities.

But it has been shown that women and members of minorities simply are not in the pool in numbers large enough to meet these hiring rates. The situation may be less critical for master's degree candidates than it is for doctorate candidates. But the aggregate projection based on the characteristics of the pool fall far short of desirable goals. Therefore, the only solution is to encourage an increase in the number of women and members of minorities in the pool and apply gradually increasing hiring rates.

It is estimated that the maximum hiring rate for women and members of minorities in the 1970s, after allowing for differences in field of specialization and type of degree, would be 35 percent and 10 percent respectively. In 1980, women would represent 28.1 percent, and members of minorities, 7.4 percent, of the full-time faculty. Assuming increased participation by women and members of minorities in the graduate schools, the hiring rate for women could be increased to 45 percent,

CHART B-5   Increasing the participation of women and members of minorities on college and university faculties, 1970–2000 (full-time faculty with differential hiring rates)

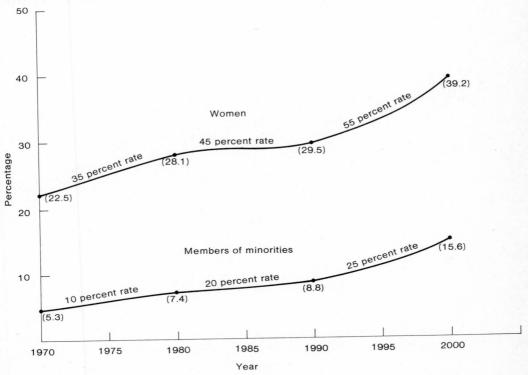

and for members of minorities to 20 percent, in the 1980s. Thus, in 1990, women would account for 29.5 percent of full-time faculty, and members of minorities would amount to 8.8 percent. It should be noted that, as the total number of faculty members declines in the middle 1980s, the percentage of women and members of minorities would remain almost constant, because the assumptions in Chart B-5 would tend to increase the numbers of younger women and members of minorities, thereby decreasing their attrition. In the 1990s, if the rates were expanded to 55 percent for women and 25 percent for members of minorities, women would comprise 39.2 percent of the full-time faculty and members of minorities, 15.6 percent by the year 2000 (Chart B-5). The effect of these hiring rates on majority males is illustrated in Chart B-6. Over the three decades, the percentage of new hires that would be majority males declines from 58.5 percent in the 1970s to 44 percent in the 1980s to 33.8 percent in the 1990s. Overall, the proportion

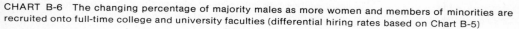

CHART B-6   The changing percentage of majority males as more women and members of minorities are recruited onto full-time college and university faculties (differential hiring rates based on Chart B-5)

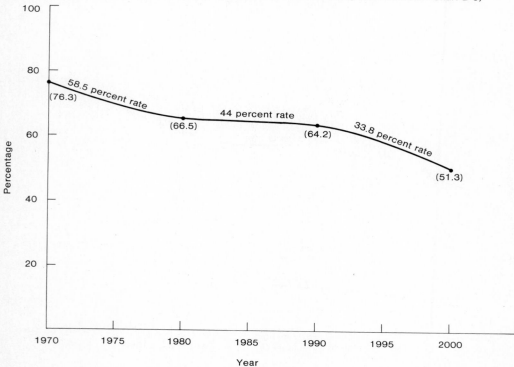

of majority males would diminish from 76.3 percent of the full-time faculty in 1970 to 51.3 percent in 2000.

The above figures illustrate what would have to be done *if* the goals we have suggested are to be accomplished by the year 2000. It may not be reasonable, or perhaps even possible, for hiring rates for women and members of minorities in the 1990s to reach the percentages indicated. If so, attainment of the proposed goals will need to wait until even later years.

PART-TIME FACULTY

The missing element in the previous discussion is part-time faculty. This group has been omitted largely because the available data about it is rather unreliable and conflicting. It is obvious, however, that much more flexibility exists for hiring part-time faculty—particularly during periods of tight budgets and uncertain enrollments. And this may be one attractive way of recruiting more women onto college and university faculties. But the inclusion of part-time faculty in discussions concerning the representation of women and members of minorities will not greatly alter the trend. As Chart B-7 shows, the percentage

CHART B-7   Women as a percentage of all faculty, 1940–1970

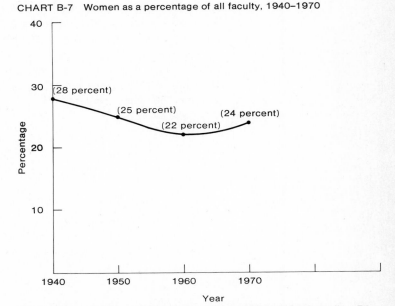

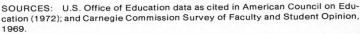

SOURCES: U.S. Office of Education data as cited in American Council on Education (1972); and Carnegie Commission Survey of Faculty and Student Opinion, 1969.

of the total faculty, including estimates of part-time faculty, representing women declined perceptibly since 1940. The 24 percent figure for 1970 is only 1.5 percent higher than the percentage representing full-time women faculty members. Similar data is unavailable for members of minorities, but there is no reason to assume that such persons constitute a disproportionately higher segment of part-time faculty. In addition, theoretical considerations would suggest that the purpose of affirmative action goes beyond mere head counting, and the nature of part-time faculty members is such that many are excluded from the traditional rights and responsibilities afforded their full-time colleagues.

CONCLUSION

Projections dealing with the future of higher education are risky. Uncertainties about enrollment, societal demands, and the development of new methods for teaching will doubtless affect the needs for new faculty. The course of college and university development may be quite different looking backward from the year 2000 than it is looking forward from the 1970s. Nevertheless, the way is clear to increase the proportions of those traditionally underrepresented on faculties. But it will take a major effort in the graduate schools, and it will require constant reevaluation of hiring practices. It will also force many to confront rather uncomfortable realities. Above all, there is very little time to make the necessary adjustments. For without the effort today, "10 years too late" could easily become "30 years too late."

REFERENCES

American Council on Education: *A Fact Book on Higher Education,* Washington, D.C., 1972.

Balderston, F. E., and Roy Radner: *Academic Demand for New Ph.D.'s, 1970–90: Its Sensitivity to Alternate Policies,* Ford Foundation for Research in University Administration, Berkeley, Calif., 1971. (Mimeographed.)

Carnegie Commission on Higher Education: *New Students and New Places: Policies for the Future Growth and Development of American Higher Education,* McGraw-Hill Book Company, New York, 1971.

Carnegie Commission on Higher Education: *College Graduates and Jobs: Adjusting to a New Labor Market Situation,* McGraw-Hill Book Company, New York, 1973.

Carnegie Commission Survey of Faculty and Student Opinion, Martin Trow, director, Berkeley, Calif., 1969.

Cartter, Allan M.: "Faculty Needs and Resources in American Higher Education," *The Annals of the American Academy of Political and Social Science,* vol. 404, pp. 71–87, November 1972.

Cartter, Allan M.: "The Academic Labor Market," in Margaret Gordon (ed.), *Higher Education and the Labor Market,* McGraw-Hill Book Company, New York, forthcoming.

Manpower Report of the President, 1972, U.S. Government Printing Office, Washington, D.C., 1972.

U.S. Bureau of the Census: "Educational Attainment: March 1972," *Current Population Reports,* ser. P-20, no. 243, 1972.

U.S. Bureau of the Census: "Persons of Spanish Origin in the United States: March 1972 and 1971," *Current Population Reports,* ser. P-20, no. 250, 1973.

EARLIER AND CONCURRENT COMMISSIONS STUDYING HIGHER EDUCATION

TECHNICAL NOTE

The performance of higher education has become an increasingly significant public concern in the United States since World War II. The period has been marked by the persistence of volatile societal issues, a growing number of students enrolled in colleges and universities, and the expenditure of more and more tax dollars on public higher education. The emergence of mass higher education, the financial crisis of the early 1950s, the rapid expansion of research and development after the launching of Sputnik, campus unrest in the 1960s, and, more recently, financial exigencies that have affected almost all our colleges and universities have occasioned thoughtful reappraisals of higher education's goals, performance, and priorities.

To engage in these reappraisals, a number of commissions—both national and local—were formed. Their reports have contributed to an understanding not only of the problems themselves, but also of possible solutions.

In this Technical Note, we examine, in particular, the reports of the following commissions:

1 The report of the President's Commission on Higher Education, George F. Zook, chairman, 1947

2 The report of the Commission on Financing Higher Education, John D. Millett, executive director, 1952

3 The report of the President's Committee on Education Beyond the High School, Devereaux C. Josephs, chairman, 1957

We also examine, in less detail, the major themes of the following commissions:

The American Council on Education Special Committee on Campus Tensions, Sol M. Linowitz, chairman, 1970

The Assembly on University Goals and Governance, Martin Meyerson, chairman, 1971

The Commission on Academic Tenure, William R. Keast, chairman, 1973

The Commission on Non-Traditional Study, Samuel B. Gould, chairman, 1973

NOTE: This technical note was prepared by John A. Ferguson of the staff of the Carnegie Commission on Higher Education.

The National Advisory Commission on Civil Disorders, Otto Kerner, chairman, 1968

The President's Commission on Campus Unrest, William W. Scranton, chairman, 1970

The U.S. Office of Education Task Force on Higher Education, Frank Newman, chairman, 1971

The White House Conference on Youth, Robben W. Fleming, chairman, Task Force on Education, 1971

It is hoped that this brief survey[1] will help to place into broader perspective the Carnegie Commission's recommendations concerning the changing problems of higher education.

THE PRESIDENT'S COMMISSION ON HIGHER EDUCATION

In the summer of 1946, President Harry S. Truman noted that, because vast numbers of veterans were entering college, institutions of higher education faced an uncertain future of strained resources. He said that the federal government would take all practicable steps to assist these institutions and to assure that all qualified veterans would have the opportunity to continue their educations. To accomplish this, he concluded that "we should now re-examine the system of higher education in terms of its objectives, methods, and facilities; and in light of the social role it has to play" (Zook, vol. 1, p. v). Accordingly, Mr. Truman appointed a special Presidential Commission on Higher Education[2] composed of 27 civic and educational leaders, and chaired by George F. Zook.

The commission began its work in the fall of 1946 and completed its task in December of 1947. Officially charged with examining the functions of higher education in the United States and the means by which they could best be performed, the commission divided its task into five major areas: (1) the

[1] There are many other studies not discussed here. In addition to many state and institutional commissions, several Presidential commissions, such as those chaired respectively by John Gardner, William Friday, Alan Pifer, and James Hester, have studied the problems of higher education. Some studies, such as those of the U.S. Office of Education Task Force on Higher Education and the Committee for Economic Development, are ongoing; some, such as *The Role of the Federal Government in Financing Higher Education* by Alice M. Rivlin (1961), operated from a limited base of interest.

[2] The President's Commission on Higher Education, George F. Zook, chairman: *Higher Education for American Democracy*, 6 vols., U.S. Government Printing Office, Washington, D.C., 1947. Hereafter cited as *Zook*.

goals of higher education; (2) the equalization and expansion of individual opportunity; (3) the organization of higher education; (4) the staffing of higher education; and (5) the financing of higher education—with the recommendations for the latter four areas dependent upon the commission's conclusions in the first.

The underlying theme of the commission's report stemmed from transformations in American society that occurred immediately after World War II. Because of a more complex national economy, with its increased production and resources, more people began to feel the need for higher education—and enrollments began to rise rapidly. Concurrently, the need for natural resources diversified under the impacts of technological advancement; a critical need developed to reconcile the economic, cultural, and religious tensions within a pluralistic society; American foreign policy shifted from isolationism to a new sense of world responsibility; and the uncertain future of the nuclear age raised new questions about the prospects of American youth. For all these reasons, the idea that new kinds of students should be accommodated gained currency. And the commission established its general theme: "Thus American colleges and universities face the need both for improving the performance of their traditional tasks and for assuming the new tasks created for them by the new internal conditions and external relations under which the American people are striving to live and to grow as a free people" (Zook, vol. 1, pp. 2–3).

The Goals of Higher Education: General Recommendations The first major concern of the commission's report was the purposes of higher education. Recognizing the principle of diversity, the commission asserted that each institution should make its own contribution in its own way, but that educational leaders should try to agree on "common objectives that can serve as a stimulus and guide to individual decision and action" (Zook, vol. 1, p. 6). There was, however, a need for a better understanding of the aims of higher education that had reached crisis proportions. The commission outlined four principles upon which the higher educational community could build a unity of purpose with a diversity of effort.

First, education should contribute to a "better nation and a better world." Institutions of higher education should make every effort toward a fuller realization of democracy. In order to preserve democracy, it must be improved; and in order to improve it, democracy must enter into every phase of college life—and not be merely a subject of study in history and political science courses. This position implied the need for a general and continuing review of institutional governance to assure that students could learn about democracy by participating in democratic processes on the campus. To contribute to a better world, colleges and universities should help to improve international understanding and cooperation. The diffusion of many ideas and cultures were largely ignored on American campuses because they emphasized the traditions of Western civilization. ideas and cultures was largely ignored on American campuses prepare students for world citizenship. In sum, higher education must help solve social problems, and it must prepare students for a responsible role in a modern society and in a modern world.

Second, the commission asserted that education should be for all Americans. But it noted five barriers to equal opportunity to pursue postsecondary education:

■ Higher education was sorely underfunded. Expenditures on colleges and universities amounted to only one-half of 1 percent of the gross national product in 1947

■ Many students simply could not afford to go to college.

■ The numbers and types of institutions varied in different areas of the country because of diverse economic conditions, and in some areas there were not enough student places.

■ A restrictive curriculum did not answer the divergent needs of potential students.

■ Outright segregation and religious quotas existed in many colleges and universities.

To alleviate these conditions, the commission recommended: increased financial support from all sources, including federal assistance to equalize regional differences; the elimination of segregation and religious quotas; diversity in curriculum; a minimum high school education for all normal students; education through the 14th grade at public expense; massive financial aid to students in grades 10 through 14; a lowering of tuition in public colleges and universities with no tuition charges for the first two years; and an increased emphasis on adult education. Further, the commission predicted that higher education enrollments would climb to 4.6 million students by 1960, with graduate enrollments rising at a rate of 170 percent. These predictions were based on the belief that at least 49 percent of eligible-age young people should attend school through the 14th grade, and 32 percent should attend school through college graduation. On this basis, the commission called for universal equal access to postsecondary education.

Third, the commission emphasized that education should contribute to the general quality of life. All too often, liberal education had been splintered by increased specialization. The commission recommended that colleges and universities adopt a unified concept of general education. General education would contribute to critical thinking, vocational pursuits, family life, an enjoyment of culture, improved health, emotional and social adjustment, an understanding and expression of ideas, and scientific discovery for modern life. With such education, students would understand better the interdependence of nations, would participate more often in solving social problems, and would assume enlarged personal and civic responsibility. To accomplish this, colleges and universities would have to discard the distinctions between general and vocational education and to incorporate extracurricular activities in a unified concept of total education.

Fourth, the commission asserted that education must be adjusted to specific social needs. Community colleges, carefully planned on a state-by-state basis, should provide cultural and educational services to local communities. They should offer semiprofessional and vocational programs—including general education—and their curricula should be regarded as terminal. Liberal arts colleges should resist specialization in order to provide for broader fields of concentration and for well-rounded graduates. Professional schools should remove quotas and restrictions imposed by the professions, and they should incorporate general education into their curriculum as much as possible. The commission saw a critical shortage of personnel, particularly in the health professions, by 1960 because of restrictions on student admissions. Overcoming these problems would require statesmanship by leaders of the professions; it also called for a continuing review of professional schools.

The commission concluded that graduate schools were badly in need of reform. It called for an increase in funds for basic research and for graduate fellowships and urged business and industry to provide broad rather than special purpose grants. It said secret research should be restricted to projects of extreme and sensitive national importance, and more research should be undertaken in the social sciences. Above all, the graduate schools should train teachers who would not only maintain scholarly interests, but would have a passionate concern for the improvement of social conditions.

Adult education should be of equal importance as traditional education in all institutions. Each college and university should become a "community college" offering services to the local community. In addition, more effort should be spent on developing audio and visual aids in the teaching process. Toward this end, the commission recommended the establishment of a commission on technical aids.

Thus, the commission set forth the broad purpose of higher education: an expanded social role for higher education that would not only strengthen and improve democracy, but would also lead to world order and peace. In this spirit, the commission made specific recommendations for the future.

The Expansion of Equal Opportunity "The swift movement of events and the growing complexity of our national life and of world affairs make it imperative, at the earliest possible time, to translate our democratic ideal into a living reality; to eliminate the barriers to equality of educational opportunity; and to expand our colleges and universities to assure that the only factors which limit enrollment are the ability and interest of the prospective students" (Zook, vol. 2, p. 1).

Asserting that the denial of educational opportunity sorely restricts the preparation of individuals for effective living, and that a democracy critically needs an informed citizenry, the commission concluded that equal access to higher education must become one of the nation's highest priorities. This could only be if a concerted effort were made to eliminate economic barriers and discrimination, and to provide financial assistance to students and more educational opportunities for adults.

With respect to economic barriers, the commission noted that a student's ability to attend college very often depended upon his parents' level of income. Moreover, because jobs for high school graduates were relatively attractive and the costs of attending college were relatively high, many able students from low-income families were unable to attend.

The commission therefore recommended the elimination of tuition during the 13th and 14th years of education, and reduced tuition beyond these years in public institutions. The responsibility for these policies was to have been shared on the local, state, and national levels of government.

The commission also recommended that institutions of higher learning become pioneers against discrimination and for tolerance. Since equal access was the right of all citizens, the commission urged that:

Legislation be passed ending discrimination

Religious quotas and other ratios be avoided

More opportunities be created for women

Questions relating to religion, color, and national or racial origins be removed on admissions, registration, and other forms

Institutions, particularly professional schools, adopt more flexible admissions policies

This would produce an educational system tuned to the concept of social justice.

Despite the commission's recommendations for lower tuitions, it perceived that economic barriers would not be lifted adequately without a program of direct assistance to students. The commission did not favor loans, citing the low usage of available loan funds in the past and the problems of incurring debt at a time when a young graduate must begin professional practice, start a family, or assume other responsibilities. Loan programs, wisely administered, could help some students, but could never, by themselves, alleviate the enormous financial difficulties associated with establishing equal access. The commission concluded that a general program of national scholarships, based on financial need, was the answer. It estimated that a program similar to the G.I. Bill could benefit approximately 20 percent of nonveteran undergraduates by providing them with $800 per year for educational expenses at an institution of their choice. Graduate students would be entitled to grants amounting to $1,500 per year. The commission justified such a program on the grounds that it was in the national interest to provide for an educated citizenry.

Finally, the commission recommended that colleges and universities assume a greater responsibility for equalizing opportunity through adult education.

The Organization of Higher Education   Colleges and universities in the United States developed without any externally imposed pattern or design, yet they depend upon government support in a number of ways. The Presidential Commission on Higher Education recognized the strength that accrued to higher education in the absence of external control, but it also recognized the need for coordination. Two general principles undergirded the commission's recommendations relating to organization: (1) uniformity has no place in a democracy, and (2) variety and flexibility should be the hallmarks of organizational patterns.

The commission recommended the development of more facilities at all levels of higher education. In particular, the commission urged that states plan for more community colleges under local control, which would provide adult education programs alternating work and school, and a well-integrated general and vocational education. If necessary, legislation was to be enacted to implement these programs.

Also, the commission recommended that the states should exercise the major responsibility for higher education, primarily through a state board of education.

The role of the federal government was to cooperate with the state agencies, to disseminate information concerning employment and educational opportunities, to assure equality of opportunity, and to assist higher education in international affairs. To do this, the commission recommended that the U.S. Office of Education be strengthened and its status be raised, and that an interdepartmental committee be established to coordinate federal activities relating to higher education.

Finally, the commission recommended that the federal government should facilitate the development of voluntary agencies that would cooperate with state agencies to examine such matters as quality of education in the lower division, educational and vocational guidance, and adult education.

The Staffing of Higher Education   Expanding enrollments in higher education created a critical need for increasing the number of competent faculty members. Increasing faculty competence was also important because the commission concluded that the quality of education could be no better than the quality of those who staff educational institutions. "Meeting this obligation will involve sustained efforts at improving the teacher's mastery of a constantly expanding subject matter field, and elevating his competence in presenting his materials" (Zook, vol. 4, p. ix). The commission recommended broad reform in four areas.

First, the commission recommended that graduate education be revamped to provide competent faculty for a changing system of higher education. Graduate education, extending three years beyond the bachelor's degree, was to provide a student with broad scholarship and special competencies, a unified knowledge of a core program, and a solid basis for future growth and development. Beyond that, the commission urged that emphasis be placed on teaching skills; that the program be suited to individual student needs; and that internships in student personnel, faculty, and administration posts be widely accepted.

Second, the commission encouraged faculty members to stimulate students to enter college teaching. To achieve that aim, the commission urged that fellowships be offered to students who wish to pursue a career in higher education; that institutions create criteria and use internships as a means of selecting and recruiting potential faculty; and that a national clearinghouse on employment in higher education be established.

Third, the commission asserted that inservice education for faculty members was sorely needed. Such programs would include group work and study, intervisitation of the classroom by colleagues, student evaluation of faculty performance, and directed teaching opportunities.

Fourth, the commission recommended vast improvements in working conditions. It particularly cited the importance of improved beginning salaries; early increases in salary; promotion based on merit; an overall salary schedule that would reflect reasonable living standards; faculty participation in academic governance; strong principles of academic freedom and tenure; and reduced student-faculty ratios.

The Financing of Higher Education The commission concluded its task by recommending a permanently expanded federal role in financing higher education. The commission listed high-quality instruction as the number one priority followed by increased resources for libraries and for research in the social sciences.

By retaining their tax exempt status and increasing the amount of private gifts for their support, the commission concluded that institutions in the private sector would manage reasonably well through 1960. The public sector, however, would operate at a deficit because of free tuition in the lower levels and low tuition in the upper levels, because local public support would not grow rapidly enough, because support would vary from state to state, and because the public institutions would absorb most of the expanding enrollments. This deficit, the commission asserted, could only be offset through federal sources.

The commission therefore recommended that the federal government create, in addition to a national scholarship program, state equalization grants, grants for construction of instructional facilities, and loans for construction of noninstructional facilities. This would account for one-third of the funds needed for the expansion of higher education to 1960. The remaining two-thirds was to be provided by state and local sources.

The final role of the federal government would be to contract for specific services, to dispense financial aid directly to students; to provide general and capital grants to public institutions, to assure accountability of expended funds, to leave administration and control to the states, and to assure universal equal access to a well-rounded education. This would be a sound pattern of continuing federal support, and it would require a continuing study of the needs and resources of higher education. In short, it would be a role of partnership in the responsibility for "attaining the goals for higher education in a democracy" (Zook, vol. 5, p. 63).

THE COMMISSION ON FINANCING HIGHER EDUCATION

In 1948, an exploratory committee on the financing of higher education recommended the establishment of a commission by the Rockefeller Foundation "to make an extensive report on the financial condition of higher education" (Millett, p. viii). In 1949, the trustees of the foundation, joined by the Carnegie Corporation of New York, granted funds to the Association of American Universities for the purpose of creating the Commission on Financing Higher Education.[3] The president of the

---

[3] The Commission on Financing Higher Education, John D. Millett, executive director: *Nature and Needs of Higher Education*, Columbia University Press, New York, 1952. Hereafter cited as *Millett*.

association selected five persons for membership on the commission, and these five added seven more to bring the total membership to twelve. John D. Millett was appointed executive director of the project. The commission began its work in the summer of 1949 and issued its report in the summer of 1952.

The commission viewed its task in terms of the general status of American higher education, its economic problems, and possible solutions to these problems for future development. Accordingly, the commission divided its report into four main topics: (1) the nature of higher education, (2) diversity in higher education, (3) economic problems, and (4) sources of financial support. Underpinning these topics was the major theme that higher education held basic and far-reaching values for American society and that its remarkable diversity in structure and in outlook ought to be preserved and strengthened.

General Considerations   The commission asserted that the current nature of higher education derived, in part, from two important sources: the early colleges, with their tradition of fixed knowledge, and, as the West opened, with a spirit of egalitarianism; and the more recent development of the universities with an increased emphasis on research and service. The result was a fourfold tradition, but it was a tradition fraught with difficulties:

■ Liberal education, the understanding of man's cultural heritage, was suffering from an increased specialization that threatened to cloud the virtues of faith, tolerance, and hope.

■ Professional education was expanding rapidly in terms of knowledge and interdependence among the disciplines, and this expansion would lead to greater costs.

■ Graduate study and research inherited the liberal traditions of freedom and intellectual curiosity, but applied research tended to receive more support than basic research—and basic research is a necessary precondition of applied research.

■ Public service had long been a high ideal in higher education, but providing for adult education and translating thought into action posed many questions for the future.

In all this, this commission felt that the overriding purpose of higher education was to promote our "heritage of freedom and of the contribution this freedom has made to our nation's position of power and responsibility in the world today" (Millett, p. 30).

Turning to students, the commission asserted that higher education should be limited to those students with the incentive and intellectual equipment to benefit from it. Attendance in higher education should not be compulsory. The commission divided learning goals into two parts: (1) the *common,* primarily a function of elementary and secondary education, improves literacy and social competence; (2) the *intellectual,* primarily the function of higher education, develops the capacities of those with unusual talent.

Diversity   The commission strongly affirmed that freedom was the basis for establishing goals in higher education and concluded that diversity was the means by which such freedom was secured. Quite simply, freedom implied the presence of choice, and choice, in turn, depended on the presence of alternatives. The commission found much diversity already present:

- In administration. Trustees, administrators, faculty, students, and alumni each had roles to play within the administrative structure.
- In choice of both teaching and learning processes.
- In support from public and private sources, which contributed to variety in control and type of institution.

Moreover, diversity bred a healthy competition among the different institutions. The commission concluded that "Because freedom depends so intimately upon diversity, it is essential to maintain the structure of higher education much as it is now" (Millett, p. 35).

Enrollment was another matter. Investigation uncovered the startling fact that most high school students in the top academic quartile failed to graduate from high school. The commission termed this a problem for the high schools—not colleges—but it recommended that steps be taken to decrease this wastage. At the time, only 40 percent of these students were attending college. The commission believed that the goal should be raised to 80 percent; and that attention to this top 25 percent in ability should become the number one priority for higher education. This was not to deny admission to students in lower quartiles, although the commission said many of them would be better served in the two-year colleges. Instead, it was to assert that more encouragement should be given to students with intellectual promise. Moreover, great diversity of interests and backgrounds existed within this group of students.

Freedom depended upon diversity, the commission concluded, and the structure of higher education, loosely organized and without centralized planning, yielded such diversity. However, pressures to conform were increasingly evident, and the commission recommended that such pressures be resisted. Voluntary cooperation and association could be quite useful, but "where the effectiveness of a function depends so essentially upon the creativeness of those performing it, uniform methods for turning out a standardized product are specious efficiency" (Millett, p. 56).

Economic Problems   Higher education means different things to different people. As a result, it is almost axiomatic that the American system of higher education has never been adequately funded to provide all the services demanded by society. The commission cited five major pressures in the 1950s affecting the financial conditions of institutions of higher education: inflation, an expansion in educational services, fluctuating enrollments, enlarged capital needs, and uncertain sources of income. To help overcome these problems, the commission recommended:

■ More funds from all sources were needed to increase the amount spent per student. The rise in prices quite literally meant a decline in quality and in expenditures per student, because colleges and universities relied heavily on tuition and incurred high fixed costs.

■ Because of enrollment fluctuations, due, in part, to the fact that military service and college education coincide for many young men, a consistent and long-range national manpower policy was sorely needed. Such a policy would help to use the talents of Americans both efficiently and justly.

■ Colleges and universities should carefully consider expanding their services. Research should be balanced between the sciences and the humanities. Moreover, institutions should accept only appropriate sponsored research projects, charging full costs, and retaining administrative flexibility for strength and integrity.

■ More money was needed for capital expansion to reflect the rising rate of enrollment.

■ Medical schools needed more funds. Such institutions had even higher costs than other institutions of higher education, and many were operating with deficits. The schools, themselves, were urged to introduce economies through reevaluating curricula, reducing the proliferation of services, employing part-time instructors, and charging patients for services rendered.

■ Liberal arts colleges were urged to reduce the proliferation of courses, and to strengthen relations with potential sources of income.

■ General efficiency measures were urged upon all institutions to examine curricular objectives, to eliminate the "cult of coverage," to consider expanding facility usage through an extension of operating hours, to subordinate all business activities to educational functions, and to explore means by which institutions could share resources.

In conclusion, the commission stated that, while higher education was not headed for bankruptcy, harmful retrenchment was taking place. Higher education had not fully shared in America's prosperity. The American people needed to be informed of this problem, and funds for higher education needed to be substantially increased. "That increase will be forthcoming when the American public clearly preceives the values to a free society which flow from higher education" (Millett, p. 115).

Sources of Financial Support The commission asserted that precise amounts of financial support needed by colleges and universities could not be determined since they depended on the quality and amount of education deemed necessary and on the general economic condition of the country. Since diversity in funding was considered the ultimate goal, the commission made these recommendations:

Student fees Tuition was expected to rise, and enrollments would continue to fluctuate. Scholarships should be provided from private sources, based on need. The economic barrier to higher education could be overcome through individual effort. Differential pricing according to subject-area costs was discouraged since it would penalize students in more expensive areas of study.

Endowment Endowment would remain relatively constant as a source of income. Therefore, institutions were urged to continue to manage endowments well.

State and local government Taxes clearly needed to be increased on the state and local levels. States should carefully consider providing aid to private colleges and universities, and should provide scholarships to students in both public and private institutions.

Federal government   Although the GI Bill was considered to be a positive program, the growing federal involvement could lead to undesirable federal control. "The strength of higher education is founded upon its freedom and upon our country's freedom; . . . . [This freedom] . . . cannot be protected if it becomes dependent upon any dominant support no matter how beneficent and enlightened that support may presently appear to be" (Millett, p. 158). Federal involvement was seen to decrease diversity and encourage "pork barrel" operations, particularly in matters involving subjective judgments. Therefore, there should be no new programs of direct federal aid to institutions or to students.

Alumni   Institutions were urged to develop alumni support, and governments were asked to increase the deduction limit for gifts in income tax returns.

Businesses, unions, and churches   These were seen as the great untapped sources of support. To be sure, these groups had participated well in the past, but the possibilities for the future, particularly for scholarship donations, loomed large.

Foundations   The commission reported that foundations often failed to provide funds for the liberal arts; little follow-up on projects occurred; research objectives were often too rigidly fixed; and many research projects were financed at less than full cost. Consequently, foundations and colleges and universities were urged to collaborate more extensively on the problems of higher education and the possible solutions to these problems.

The surrounding community   Institutions were urged to cooperate with the surrounding community to establish an awareness of mutual advantages and responsibilities.

The financial plight of higher education called for immediate action, and, on the one hand, the commission recommended that all institutions take steps to ensure that their resources were being used effectively. On the other hand, it said that increased financial support had to be provided from all sources. "But adequacy of support is not our sole concern. Higher education must continue to have varied and diverse support if it is to be free and if it is to reflect the fundamental characteristics of a society which is free" (Millett, p. 6).

THE PRESIDENT'S COMMITTEE ON EDUCATION BEYOND THE HIGH SCHOOL

In the spring of 1956, President Dwight D. Eisenhower established a Committee on Education Beyond the High School[4] "charged with three tasks: 'to lay before us all' the problems of education beyond the high school, 'to encourage active and systematic attack' on the problems, and 'to develop, through studies and conferences, proposals in this educational field'" (Josephs, vol. 2, p. ix). The committee consisted of 35 educators and lay persons, and it was chaired by Devereaux C. Josephs. It issued its final report in the summer of 1957.

The committee issued an interim report in 1956, however, that outlined the major areas of concern, and that listed its preliminary conclusions. Following this report, the committee singled out certain areas for further study: the need for faculty, financial aid to students, educational opportunity, financing, and the role of the federal government. Within each of these areas, the committee made specific recommendations for the future of postsecondary education.

General Considerations   From the preliminary conclusions of the committee's *First Interim Report* came the premises upon which the recommendations were made in its *Second Report.* The six preliminary conclusions were:

1   Our ideals and the increasing complexity of our civilization require that each individual develop his or her talents to the fullest.

2   The needs of the individual and of society plus an unprecedented growth in the population of post-high school age will far outrun the present or planned capacity of existing colleges and universities and other post-high school institutions.

3   The needs of the oncoming millions of individuals with varying capacities and interests will call for a broader range of educational opportunities, and less rigid time requirements.

4   Many more able and qualified teachers will be needed than present efforts can provide.

---

[4]The President's Committee on Education Beyond the High School, Devereaux C. Josephs, chairman: *First Interim Report to the President,* U.S. Government Printing Office, Washington, D.C., 1956; and *Second Report to the President,* U.S. Government Printing Office, Washington, D.C., 1957. Hereafter cited as *Josephs.*

5 There must be promptly formulated an explicit, considered policy of the role of the federal government in education beyond the high school.

6 Even with the best possible utilization of existing resources, additional financial support must be provided if the additional millions in the population are to be enabled to develop their talents to the fullest (Josephs, vol. 1, pp. 6–11).

The basic premises listed in the *Second Report* were:

1 We are concerned, as individuals and as a nation, with promoting the fullest possible development of the aptitudes and abilities of our population.

2 Our ideals and the increasing complexity of our civilization require that each individual, regardless of race, creed, color, or national origin, have the opportunity to pursue educational training beyond high school to the full extent for which he or she is willing or able.

3 The needs and demands of individuals and of society in the next ten to fifteen years will require great expansion of the overall capacity of existing colleges and universities and of other post-high school institutions, with improvement rather than sacrifice of quality. Greater diversity and accessibility of educational opportunities will also be needed.

4 The key figure in the educational equation is the teacher. Many more teachers both able and highly qualified will be needed. Substantial salary increases are imperative.

5 There must be a clarification of responsibilities for providing the needed additional financial support to both institutions and individuals.

6 The proper role of the federal government in post-high school education needs to be determined (Josephs, vol. 2, pp. ix–x).

The Need for Faculty One of the most acute and immediate problems facing higher education in 1956, according to the President's committee, was the growing shortage of qualified teachers. The committee estimated that between 180,000 and 270,000 new college teachers would be needed over the next dozen years. Recommendations of the committee attacked the problem from four different angles:

1 Improving economic benefits for the faculty. The committee recommended that governing boards and legislatures give

high priority to increased salaries for faculty members, thereby attracting more qualified teachers to the profession while eliminating low faculty salaries as a "hidden subsidy" to higher education. The committee set the goal of doubling the average salary level within 5 to 10 years. In addition, institutions were urged to enhance the attractiveness of the profession by providing moderate-cost housing and increased fringe benefits.

2 Improving the mechanisms for recruiting. The committee recommended that each institution of higher education cooperate with national associations in an effort to locate talent for its faculty, and that more women be brought into the profession. Such efforts could be enhanced through the work of national clearinghouses supported by private foundations.

3 Using teacher time more efficiently. The committee believed that all faculties should regularly review their own curricula in the light of changing student needs and institutional resources. The committee also felt that institutions should increase their effectiveness and productiveness by employing new instructional technologies and other procedures that rely more on self-education; by adapting class sizes more efficiently; and by reducing the nonteaching duties of faculty members through greater use of assistants.

4 Strengthening the graduate school. The committee discouraged the proliferation of courses in colleges and universities and hoped that periodic reviews would help slow the trend toward overspecialization. Nevertheless, it viewed the strengthening of graduate schools as a prerequisite to increasing the supply of college teachers. Thus the committee urged universities to expand their graduate schools in all major fields, to devise new programs for the preparation of college teachers, and to offer financial assistance to their best students.

Financial Aid to Students To make higher education more readily accessible to all individuals with the ability to pursue it, the committee recommended elimination of discrimination, greater use of interstate compacts, expansion of guidance and counseling services, coordination of informational services, and greater research on factors relating to drop outs.

In addition, the committee made five recommendations designed to provide various forms of financial assistance to students. They included encouragement of private loans at low interest rates to be repaid after the student graduated, a federally funded work-study program providing jobs for 25,000 to 50,000 students per year, proposals for tax benefits through deductions or credits for college expenses, and encouragement for more private, local, and state scholarship funds. A federal scholarship program for undergraduates was recommended only if absolutely necessary after further experience with other scholarship fund sources. If there was to be a federal program, the committee urged that it be accompanied by cost-of-education grants to the institutions for students receiving scholarships.

Expansion and Diversity With respect to planning, the committee was concerned with maximum use of existing institutions, caution in the development of community colleges, and greater understanding of adult education and education within business and industry.

The committee asserted that an increasing number of students could be accommodated economically by expanding existing institutions as a first step. It was felt that the creation of new institutions would detract from the services and resources of existing ones. While it recognized that community colleges had particular merits in meeting the increased demand for education, the committee nonetheless urged caution in expansion of junior colleges, especially insofar as unsound planning might lead to an unnecessarily large burden on scarce community resources. Many colleges were already considered too small to be economical. In two other areas—education in industry and adult education generally—the committee did not make specific recommendations, but rather recommended that there be further study of these areas to determine the most desirable relationship between them and other sectors of postsecondary education.

In short, the committee believed that careful planning and diversity of institutions were the basis for strength in education beyond the high school. Such planning, moreover, should transcend state boundaries and should allow for an expanded federal involvement. While diversity was important, primarily because of differing needs within a complex society, only careful planning could assure that a common denominator of adaptability, founded in the basic skills, would exist for students.

Financing The committee based its recommendations for financing higher education on the assumption that total enrollment in higher education would expand to 6 million in 1970 and that total operational costs would double. Observing that approximately 0.68 percent of the gross national product for 1953–54 was spent for educational and general expenditures of higher education in the United States, the committee predicted that by 1970 between 1.01 and 1.10 percent of the GNP would be required for these purposes. The recommendations centered around four areas of concern.

1   To finance higher education. The committee did not recommend major federal aid. Instead it recommended increased support from states, local governments, business and industry, and private donors encouraged by tax credits. In addition, the committee recommended that tuition charges in public institutions be increased no faster than the rate of increase of family discretionary income; that private institutions increase tuition to maintain the proportion of total costs then paid by students; and that financial assistance be increased to meet increases in tuition charges.

2   To increase efficient use of resources. Concerned with the general need for increasing the efficiency with which colleges and universities used their available resources, the committee recommended that worthy small colleges be encouraged to expand and achieve accreditation; that the states disseminate to the high schools information regarding freshman openings in various institutions; that more attention be paid to efficiency in management practices through clearinghouses and inter-institutional cooperation; and that the federal government develop equitable policies for payment for services rendered by colleges and universities.

3   To expand facilities. The committee was generally opposed to programs of federal aid to institutions, but aid for construction was the notable exception. In proposing federal funds for construction of classrooms, laboratories, and other nonprofit-producing facilities, the committee made no distinction between publicly and privately controlled institutions. It did insist that such grants be made only in amounts matched by the institutions or state and local governments. The committee noted that the requirement for capital outlay through 1970 was likely to be approximately $1.3 billion per year. It did not indicate what percentage of this proportion should come from federal sources.

4   To facilitate planning. The committee recommended that essential data on the costs of higher education be immediately developed by the U.S. Office of Education and that institutions make the public aware of the real costs. In facing the problems of financing higher education, the committee established the following priorities:

In general:

■ Payment of salaries sufficient to retain and compensate adequately, and to attract the needed additional numbers of teachers of high ability.

■ Provision of faculties and facilities needed to assure maintenance of quality, and expanded and strengthened graduate programs for college teacher preparation.

■ Provision for assistance to students to ensure that the best talent is included in the increasing enrollments and that all qualified persons have appropriate educational opportunity (Josephs, vol. 2, p. 88).

Each institution should:

■ Undertake immediately, if it has not already done so, an intensive and imaginative study of its long-range goals and plans, with particular attention to its future size.

■ Avoid physical expansion at the expense of diverting funds from needed faculty salary increases.

■ Plan all new construction carefully in relation to the prospective needs of its area and in coordination with neighboring institutions.

■ Ensure that maximum use is being made of present facilities before building new ones (Josephs, vol. 2, p. 89).

The Role of the Federal Government   The committee observed that relationships between the federal government and postsecondary education were not only exceedingly complex, but were nowhere centrally or adequately recorded. Furthermore, the committee questioned whether the $1 billion in federal aid then available to postsecondary education was properly referred to as *aid* and suggested that some of this money consisted of only partial payment for services requested by the government.

The committee's recommendations concerning the federal

government were designed so that the government would facilitate planning, aid higher education without controlling it, and provide continuing advisory groups.

In its first recommendation under this heading, the committee outlined the role it believed the federal government should assume:

The Federal Government should provide broad national leadership, should collect and provide useful data and services, and should provide certain other needed assistance, such as is recommended in this Report. But it should do these things only by methods which strengthen State and local effort and responsibility and, in the case of direct financial assistance, only through programs which are periodically reviewed and which are promptly terminated when no longer clearly justifiable. Finally, the Federal Government should studiously avoid programs and policies which carry the threat either of control or of other adverse effects upon the educational institutions (Josephs, vol. 2, p. 106).

In particular, the committee recommended that the federal government:

■ Increase fact-finding and reporting services in the same sense as such services are rendered to farmers and business-men

■ Provide technical and professional assistance to institutions and states engaged in educational planning

■ Encourage experimentation and innovation

■ Establish a continuing interagency coordinating committee and an advisory committee composed of laymen and educators

The President's Committee on Higher Education established the urgent priority of improving educational opportunity beyond the high school through programs requiring federal, state, and local action spurred by careful planning and coordination. But it also recognized the need to preserve diversity: "The great diversity of our educational establishment provides the opportunity for a variety of plans and experiments. They should be encouraged" (Josephs, vol. 2, p. xii).

THE AMERICAN COUNCIL ON EDUCATION
SPECIAL COMMITTEE ON CAMPUS TENSIONS

In June 1969, the board of directors of the American Council on Education established a Special Committee on Campus Tensions[5] composed of lay leaders and spokesmen from various segments of the higher education community to study campus tensions and to suggest remedies to institutions of higher education. Operating in a period of widespread disruption on the nation's campuses, the committee undertook to study ways in which the higher education community could solve its own problems and thereby thwart such punitive measures as reduced financial support, harmful and restrictive legislation, and political intervention into internal institutional affairs.

The committee addressed each broad segment of higher education individually, and the major themes of their recommendations can be summarized as follows:

Students   The committee believed that students should have autonomy in nonacademic student affairs and that they should have increased participation in the academic affairs of the institution—particularly in curricular matters.

Faculty   The committee recommended that the faculty should reassert its influence over the academic affairs of the institution, and that more emphasis should be placed on effective teaching.

Administrators   The committee asserted that the roles of administrators should be regularly reviewed, and that responsibility should be accompanied by the necessary authority to act—particularly at the presidential level.

Trustees   The committee recommended that appointments to governing boards should be for fixed terms with greater attention given to achieving diversity among board members, and that trustees should pay more attention to educational issues and less to mere housekeeping chores.

Throughout its recommendations, the committee asserted that the key to a successful academic enterprise lay in effective and open communication among these various constituents. Such communication depended upon respect for the rights of others, the assumption of individual responsibility, and fair and well-publicized rules and regulations. To achieve these aims, the committee made a series of recommendations concerning governance and institutional goals.

Governance   The committee believed that due process and fair governance procedures should be enlarged to cover the

[5] The American Council on Education, Special Committee on Campus Tensions, Sol M. Linowitz, chairman: *Campus Tensions: Analysis and Recommendations,* American Council on Education, Washington, D.C., 1970.

entire academic community, and that academic and policy questions and grievances should be openly aired by the campus. Furthermore, through joint committees, a commitment to the principles of self-governance should be made, along with the acceptance of responsibility that such self-governance implies.

Institutional goals The committee believed that change and self-renewal would occur only through the concerted efforts of all campus constituents. But certain tangible steps could be taken immediately to encourage such change. Specifically, the committee recommended that institutions provide for diversity in the faculty and staff; respond to the educational needs of women; develop new curricula for the self-development of students; establish centers for educational research and innovation; reduce the emphasis on traditional degree structures; extend access through experimental admissions programs; establish ethnic studies programs; and concentrate efforts aimed at recruiting more minorities.

The committee asserted that campus tensions, in and of themselves, are not necessarily harmful. They often lead to constructive change on the campus. And inappropriate responses to campus turmoil can often be as harmful as those tensions that lead directly to violence and disruption. But the committee observed that the diversity in American higher education rendered a uniform diagnosis and prescription for the problems emanating from campus disorders virtually impossible.

THE ASSEMBLY ON UNIVERSITY GOALS AND GOVERNANCE

The Assembly on University Goals and Governance was established by the American Academy of Arts and Sciences[6] in September 1969 to explore alternative approaches for resolving problems affecting institutions of higher education. The report of the assembly consisted of 85 theses dealing with a broad range of topics of major concern to higher education. Woven throughout these theses were a set of assumptions or major themes:

1   The central mission of American higher education is learning.

[6] The Assembly on University Goals and Governance, Martin Meyerson, chairman: *First Report,* The American Academy of Arts and Sciences, Cambridge, Mass., 1971.

2　Since institutions of higher education must learn to scrutinize themselves in much the same way as they scrutinize other elements in our society, self-knowledge is the basis for educational reform.

3　Colleges and universities need to be more open to those who are able to benefit from educational experiences; therefore, choice in admissions and attendance must be more widely extended to such persons.

4　In both undergraduate and graduate education, experimentation and flexibility are needed to provide for new options and alternatives.

5　Both diversification and differentiation need to be preserved and extended throughout American higher education.

6　Educational diversity depends upon the preservation of the public and private systems of higher learning.

7　The professoriate should be enhanced through easier entrance and exit for more diverse segments of the population, the art of teaching should be upgraded, and an environment should be created in which learning is as important for teachers as for students.

8　To the presidency is delegated both authority and accountability; the executive function therefore needs to be strengthened.

9　In the face of continuing financial difficulties, colleges and universities should recognize that federal funds may not be readily available, and that the only solution may be to individually and collectively help themselves.

Based on these themes, the assembly issued its theses in areas that can be summarized and subdivided under six general headings:

Students　The assembly stated that access to higher education, along with more flexibility in patterns of attendance and in degree structures, needed to be extended in order to overcome past neglects to the poor, to members of minorities, and to women.

The teaching profession　The assembly recommended that faculties pay more attention to diversity in their departments, to external review and student evaluations in personnel actions, to self-regulation, and to continuing professional development.

Curriculum　The assembly called for more experimentation with new methods of teaching, a more careful definition of curricular expectations, and more flexible scheduling of course-work.

Research and service The assembly recommended the aboli-tion of secret research and the limitation of research and ser-vice to activities that contribute to the mission of the institu-tions.

Governance The assembly based its recommendations on governance on a concept of shared authority. The concept em-bodied lay boards with term appointments, a strong president exerting educational leadership, the delegation of responsi-bility, and the use of ombudsmen.

The use of resources Particularly in times of financial exigency, the assembly recommended that colleges and universities en-gage in long-range planning and budgeting, and that they share resources through interinstitutional cooperation.

THE COMMISSION ON ACADEMIC TENURE

The Commission on Academic Tenure[7] formed in 1971, was cosponsored by the American Association of University Pro-fessors and the Association of American Colleges to conduct an independent examination of tenure policies and practices in American higher education. The commission's major con-clusion was that academic tenure ought to be retained as the characteristic form for organizing professional teaching and scholarly service in American colleges and universities largely because of its paramount importance in protecting academic freedom.

The commission recognized many shortcomings in tenure practices, however, and its recommendations were addressed to specific ways of improving such practices.

Professional development The commission urged that more re-sources from institutions and associations be devoted to new teaching techniques, to the changing demands of new students, and to new developments in the disciplines.

The role of the faculty The commission believed that faculty members should undertake the primary responsibility to ensure excellence in the recommendations for promotion and the award of tenure.

Institutional regulations The commission recommended that

[7] The Commission on Academic Tenure in Higher Education, William R. Keast, chairman, *Faculty Tenure*, Jossey-Bass, Inc., San Francisco, 1973.

each institution develop a full and formal policy statement on faculty personnel policy outlining criteria for appointment and promotion.

Staff planning The commission recommended that colleges and universities should project staff requirements for the future on a regular basis in order to guide personnel decisions in light of changing programs, enrollment, budget and other resources, and institutional goals. It further asserted that most institutions should not allow more than one-half to two-thirds of their faculty to hold tenure appointments.

Collective bargaining The commission recommended that collective bargaining not extend to academic freedom and tenure and related faculty personnel matters.

Research on higher education In the belief that colleges and universities often operate without adequate information regarding personnel practices, the commission recommended that institutions and associations, on a systematic and continuing basis, conduct research and obtain the information they need in reviewing and strengthening their own policies and procedures.

The focus of the commission's report was primarily upon the individual institution in the belief that improvement was most needed there. In the end, the commission asserted, the weaknesses in the tenure system arose not from any inherent defect in the principle of tenure, but from serious deficiencies in its application and administration in individual institutions of higher education.

THE COMMISSION ON NON-TRADITIONAL STUDY

In 1971 the Educational Testing Service and the College Entrance Examination Board established the Commission on Non-Traditional Study[8] to examine the range of possibilities and the relative significance of nontraditional study and to make recommendations for the future. The commission defined *nontraditional study* as an attitude, rather than a system, that places emphasis on the student, that encourages diversity of individual effort, competence, and performance, and that deemphasizes time and space. Nontraditional study was equated with more opportunity for lifelong learning.

[8] The Commission on Non-Traditional Study, Samuel B. Gould, chairman, *Diversity by Design*, Jossey-Bass, Inc., San Francisco, 1973.

Educational opportunities Without denying the importance of traditional methods of postsecondary education, the commission recommended that a wider range of educational options be available, along with financial assistance, for young people. It also urged that increased emphasis be placed on the concept of life-long learning.

Institutional reform Asserting that rigidities of time and space often lead to elitism, the commission urged institutions of higher learning to pay more attention to the problems of articulation among various sources of learning, to engage in inter-institutional cooperation, to employ more part-time faculty with particular experiences, and to place more emphasis on learning and less on degree structures.

Alternatives The commission recommended that educators examine the use of such alternatives as public libraries and instructional technology (especially cable television and video-cassettes) in their attempts to provide more options for students. The commission further recommended the development of an inventory of local educational resources. It recommended that institutional cooperation be guided by shared purposes rather than by geographic proximity.

In addition, the commission recommended that a national registry be established to evaluate a student's accomplishments and to advise him of ways to complete a degree program; and that research on nontraditional studies be accomplished, and information be disseminated through the use of collaborative efforts, clearinghouses, and workshops. Through these various efforts, the commission concluded, all resources for learning would be marshaled to meet the educational needs of society and the individual.

THE NATIONAL ADVISORY COMMISSION ON CIVIL DISORDERS

In the summer of 1967, amidst civil disorder and rioting in many major American cities, the President of the United States issued an order creating the National Advisory Commission on Civil Disorders[9] to examine the nature and causes of civil disorder and to make recommendations dealing with the problems causing or emanating from such disorders. While the commission's

[9] The National Advisory Commission on Civil Disorders, Otto Kerner, chairman: *Report of the National Advisory Commission on Civil Disorders,* New York Times Company, New York, 1968.

report centered upon the larger society, it contained many recommendations concerning higher education. In general, it was the commission's contention that the number one priority for higher education was equal educational opportunity. It therefore asserted that the promise of educational opportunity was denied to many of our nation's disadvantaged young people.

The commission recommended:

■ The establishment of special one-year post-high school college preparatory schools to help overcome the poor level of education attained by young people from the ghettos

■ The removal of financial barriers to higher education by an expansion of grant and work-study programs

■ The implementation of a loan forgiveness feature for persons wishing to obtain a college education in order to fill needed public service jobs in disadvantaged areas

■ More funds and more emphasis on vocational education with particular concern for linking vocational education to job opportunities

The success of these endeavors, in the commission's view, would depend on the willingness of each level of government to accept the responsibility for leadership in promoting policies designed to improve integration and quality in education. More funds would be necessary from the federal government; more careful planning from the states; and more commitment from the local community. But each would depend on the others. The commission said that its recommendations were designed to upgrade the entire educational system, but until elementary and secondary education were able to assume their proper roles in providing a sound basis for the individual growth of disadvantaged youth, higher education would need to make special efforts.

THE PRESIDENT'S COMMISSION ON CAMPUS UNREST

In the wake of the tragedies at Kent State University and Jackson State University, the President of the United States established the Commission on Campus Unrest[10] in June 1970 to examine the causes of campus unrest and to make recommen-

[10] The President's Commission on Campus Unrest, William W. Scranton, chairman: *Campus Unrest*, U.S. Government Printing Office, Washington, D.C., 1970.

dations for future action. The commission immediately called for a reconciliation among the divergent voices in American society, noting that student protest in the 1960s was not necessarily new, and that the causes of campus unrest were complex.

The commission addressed recommendations to both colleges and universities and to civil authorities. Institutions of higher education were urged to be sensitive to the issues raised by the protesters; to uphold dissent, but to be willing to file charges in the case of violence; to define lawful protest and to implement fair disciplinary codes; and, during actual demonstrations, to negotiate, to wait out the protest, and to employ court-ordered injunctions. Civil authorities were urged to plan actions with colleges and universities well in advance of protests; to exercise restraint in dealing with demonstrators and demonstrations; and to employ only well-trained professionals for use in crowd-control activities.

With respect to reform in higher education, the commission asserted that each institution should state its goals and guarantee the rights of its constituents, keeping in mind that academic freedom should imply institutional neutrality. Further, colleges and universities were urged to abolish secret research, to establish guidelines for consulting activities, to cooperate with the surrounding community, and to extend educational and cultural services to off-campus constituents. Institutions should also be more flexible in scheduling courses for students by including more options for stopping out and for diversity in teaching methods; they should limit their size, decentralize wherever possible, and reconsider tenure practices. Finally, the commission recommended that governance procedures should allow for active participation by those affected by particular decisions, but administrative leadership should not be undermined in the process.

The commission addressed recommendations to each of the campus constituents:

Students   Students were urged to exercise restraint in their demands. They should remember that the function of educational institutions includes both teaching *and* research. They should realize that their demands will have some effect, even though they will not always be the basis for new policies.

Faculty   The commission recommended that faculty members be more informed of the full complexities of the college or university, and that they pay more attention to teaching performance while limiting outside service.

Administrators   The commission said that the primary role of the administration was to exercise educational leadership. Consequently, academic administrators should be able to defend and articulate the mission of the institution, and they should take steps to ensure that open channels of communication exist between themselves and the students.

Trustees   The commission recommended that the trustees be more familiar with the educational mission of the college or university, and that their main role be that of a buffer between the institution and the outside. They should recognize that an essential purpose of higher education is teaching.

Alumni   The commission cautioned alumni not to make hasty judgments about their particular institutions, but to offer constructive criticism for improvement and continued financial support for the future.

The commission called on the federal government to provide leadership at the Presidential level as a first step in preventing violence and encouraging understanding. Beyond that, it recommended that the federal government assist campuses in creating more service programs and other options for students; that the level of federal financial support be increased; and that financial aid to students not be terminated as a punitive measure for involvement in campus protest activities. Indeed, the commission addressed these recommendations to all levels of government in an effort to avoid violence in the future by strengthening American colleges and universities.

THE U.S. OFFICE OF EDUCATION TASK FORCE ON HIGHER EDUCATION

Toward the end of the 1960s, the Secretary of Health, Education, and Welfare suggested the establishment of an independent task force to study the problems facing American higher education and to make recommendations concerning the future to the U.S. Office of Education, to the higher education community, and to the general public. The Task Force on Higher Education,[11] in accepting the charge, set as its mission an analysis of how well America's system of higher education matched society's needs and interests.

The task force asserted that the foremost priority was to make possible the establishment of new educational enterprises,

[11] Task Force on Higher Education, Frank Newman, chairman: *Report on Higher Education*, U.S. Government Printing Office, Washington, D.C., 1971.

including single-mission institutions and institutions with innovative educational formats. The strategy to be employed was to
fund specific rather than general programs; to grant funds to
students and thereby create a market for specific academic
enterprises; and to add public members to accrediting organizations and reduce state and federal reliance on such organizations with respect to disbursing funds. Such steps would tend
to create a student-oriented, more flexible system of postsecondary education.

The task force gave particular attention to the following:

Patterns of attendance   The task force recommended that more
options, particularly those sponsored by business and local
government, be made available to students. Such options
should include internships and outside experiences. More
attention should also be paid to life-long learning, to employing
regional examinations, to developing "television colleges," and
to offering financial assistance to those engaged in such
pursuits.

Minority groups   It asserted that the tendency to encourage
minority groups to attend low-cost public two-year colleges
ought to be avoided. Colleges and universities should not
merely adapt but also actively encourage minority-group
participation.

Women   It called for concerted effort to provide equal access
and equal pay for women in higher education. Immediate re-
forms should include changing regulations on financial aids and
residency requirements and establishing child-care facilities
on campuses.

The faculty   It recommended that more part-time faculty members be employed and that special chairs, exempt from normal
criteria, be established in order to meet the needs of new students and new programs. Furthermore, it recommended that
promotion should be based on merit, and that tenure rules
should be revised.

Institutional goals   It recommended that institutions drop programs unrelated to their educational purposes; that each college or university examine its programs in light of its goals;
and that new institutions be established for scholarly research
and for professional training.

The task force concluded its report by asserting that major
problems remained to be examined, including: (1) the illegiti-
macy of cost effectiveness in decision making; (2) the reform of

graduate education; and (3) the overreliance on degrees as credentials.

In a later report, the task force recommended the consolidation of data-gathering activities in the Office of Education in order to more easily disseminate information to the higher education community; a "GI Bill" for community service; and the establishment of new criteria for the selection of graduate fellows.

Throughout its work, the task force called for a change in attitudes about higher education on the part of educators and lay persons alike in order to more nearly match the needs of society with the potential of the higher education community.

THE WHITE HOUSE CONFERENCE ON YOUTH

In 1971 the President of the United States appointed a National Chairman of the White House Conference on Youth[12] and charged him to plan a conference whereby the youth of America could address the issues most pressing to them. The conference provided a forum for young people, in interaction with adults in positions of authority, to discuss problems of concern to youth and to propose solutions for those problems. Much of the debate and many of the resulting recommendations pertained to higher education.

Of particular concern here is the report of the Task Force on Education whose major recommendations may be summarized as follows:

■ Federal spending priorities should be reordered so that a larger percentage will be spent on education; experimental and innovative educational systems should receive more emphasis.

■ Students should be included as voting members of policy-making bodies in colleges and universities, and codes of student rights and responsibilities should be developed.

■ Equality of opportunity should be ensured through eliminating discrimination, revamping outmoded curricula, and offering adequate assistance.

■ Alternative educational systems should be established along

[12] The White House Conference on Youth, Stephen Hess, chairman: *Report of the White House Conference on Youth;* Robben W. Fleming, chairman, Task Force on Education, U.S. Government Printing Office, Washington, D.C., 1971.

with adequate counseling services, opportunities for dropouts to return to classes, environmental programs, and more use of instructional technology.

- Colleges and universities should extend their educational and cultural facilities to the surrounding community. This should include establishing life-long community learning centers.

- Teacher training should be reformed so that the schools can center on the student as a person, rather than on subject content alone.

- The tenure system should be revamped so that faculty members are offered contracts and are evaluated on the basis of teaching performance.

- The federal government should immediately and fully fund existing programs of financial aid as an important first step.

The task force asserted that the primary goal of education should be the self-actualization of the individuals served. It called for a more humane educational system that would allow more flexibility and more options for a student to pursue his personal goals.

CONCLUSION

The foregoing sections represent a limited account of the major themes and recommendations of several of the commissions and task forces that have studied higher education in the United States. The purpose of this review is to offer perspective for the recommendations of the Carnegie Commission and to show the historical patterns of concerns and the range of solutions offered for those concerns.

One way of comparing the conclusions and recommendations of the reports summarized earlier is to pose a set of hypotheses and to examine the degree to which a commission or task force would agree with each statement. In each of the following charts, a proposition is stated, and each commission, including the Carnegie Commission, is visually represented according to whether it would give the proposition a high or a low priority. The illustrated positions on the charts are functions of three items: (1) whether the commission addressed the issue implied by the statement; (2) how important the issue was in relation to the commission's other recommendations; and (3) how important the issue was in relation to its importance for other commissions. No attempt at quantifying these positions has been made; instead, it is hoped that the relative position of each commission can be graphically and broadly portrayed and that certain trends may be discerned.

While no value judgments are implied by these charts, and while no hypothesis is a verbatim recommendation of any single commission, one can conclude that a position of strong, positive emphasis indicates a generally high level of agreement with the statement. Conversely, a position of strong or moderate opposition implies disagreement. The broad middle ground, moderate endorsement, means that the commission or task force was concerned with the issue and would have agreed with the statement in principle. A full understanding of any particular position, of course, requires that one refer to the original report of that commission or task force, since emphases and implementing recommendations vastly differ from one report to another.

Finally, some issues were not examined in detail by certain commissions and task forces. In such cases, they appear in the "Not considered" column of the appropriate chart. But although it would be inappropriate to assess the likely position of a commission on a topic not directly addressed by it, "Not considered" does not necessarily imply that the commission was unaware of the issue. For example, on Chart 4, the Commission on Academic Tenure is depicted as having not considered the issue of conserving institutional resources. While this is technically true, the commission was well aware of the scarcity of resources, since it devoted much discussion to the problems of budgeting and planning as they relate to tenure policies. Similarly, implied consideration of a specified issue can be found in other reports. But the entries on the charts, insofar as possible, correspond to the actual recommendations of the commissions and task forces.

Turning to the charts, certain observations can be made:

1   Support for increased federal financial assistance in general (Table C-1) was greatest in the Commission on Higher Education and in the White House Conference. The Commission on Financing Higher Education disagreed, in part, because of its fear of federal domination.

2   There was general agreement that equality of opportunity should be a major goal of higher education (Table C-2). Again, the Commission on Financing Higher Education sharply dis-

agreed, asserting that more efforts should be directed toward educating high-ability students.

3   The Special Committee on Campus Tensions and the Commission on Campus Unrest, both concerned with campus disorder, and the White House Conference, concerned with student participation, all placed a relatively higher degree of emphasis on the role of the trustees in educational affairs (Table C-3) than others even though there was general agreement with the statement that "trustees should be actively involved in the governance of higher education, including broad educational policy."

4   The effective use of scarce resources (Table C-4) was of major concern to the Commission on Financing Higher Education, the Carnegie Commission, and the Assembly on University Goals and Governance. These three groups studied the financing of higher education during periods of great financial instability.

5   There was strong agreement that independence and diversity ought to be preserved in American higher education (Table C-5), and general agreement that administrators should provide more educational leadership (Table C-6).

6   The primacy of the faculty in academic affairs had very high priority for the Special Committee on Campus Tensions, the Assembly on University Goals and Governance, the Commission on Academic Tenure, and the Carnegie Commission, but it also received support from virtually all other groups (Table C-7). On the other hand, there was general opposition to retaining an unchanged tenure system (Table C-8).

7   The White House Conference placed great emphasis on student participation (Table C-9); strong support with reservations was seen in several other commissions and task forces. But the Commission on Financing Higher Education and the Committee on Education Beyond the High School tended to oppose the statement inasmuch as they were far more concerned with upgrading the status of the faculty in academic affairs.

8   The Commission on Higher Education, the Carnegie Commission, and the U.S. Office of Education Task Force attached great importance to financing higher education through students, primarily to avoid external controls but also to encourage institutions to improve their programs in competition with others (Table C-10). Remarkably, the Commission on Financing

Higher Education disagreed, although it too sought to avoid outside interference in institutional affairs.

9   There was general agreement that the states should assume the major responsibility for higher education with very strong endorsements by the Commission on Higher Education and the Carnegie Commission (Table C-11), but only moderate agreement that the states should provide aid to private institutions of higher education, with the Commission on Higher Education dissenting (Table C-12).

The charts illustrate how different commissions and task forces viewed the problems then at hand. Such a time perspective may suggest why the Millett Commission and the White House Conference, for example, differed so greatly on so many issues. But, and perhaps more importantly, the charts point to the absence of universally accepted solutions to the problems confronting institutions of higher education. Differences of opinion will always exist among reasonable people in a democratic society. It is all the more remarkable, then, that at least a general consensus can be found in so many areas on so broad a range of complex issues.

TABLE C-1   "The federal government should expand its support for higher education."

	NOT CON- SIDERED	STRONG OR MODERATE OPPOSI- TION	MODERATE ENDORSE- MENT	STRONG, POSITIVE EMPHASIS
COMMISSION ON HIGHER EDUCATION, 1947				X
COMMISSION ON FINANCING HIGHER EDUCATION, 1952		X		
COMMITTEE ON EDUCATION BEYOND THE HIGH SCHOOL, 1956			X	
SPECIAL COMMITTEE ON CAMPUS TENSIONS, 1970			X	
ASSEMBLY ON UNIVERSITY GOALS AND GOVERNANCE, 1971	X			
COMMISSION ON ACADEMIC TENURE, 1973	X			
COMMISSION ON NON-TRADITIONAL STUDY, 1973	X			
COMMISSION ON CIVIL DISORDERS, 1968			X	
COMMISSION ON CAMPUS UNREST, 1970			X	
U.S. OFFICE OF EDUCATION TASK FORCE, 1971			X	
WHITE HOUSE CONFERENCE, 1971				X
CARNEGIE COMMISSION, 1973			X	

TABLE C-2 "The United States should have a system of universal access to higher education."

	NOT CONSIDERED	STRONG OR MODERATE OPPOSITION	MODERATE ENDORSEMENT	STRONG, POSITIVE EMPHASIS
COMMISSION ON HIGHER EDUCATION, 1947				x
COMMISSION ON FINANCING HIGHER EDUCATION, 1952		x		
COMMITTEE ON EDUCATION BEYOND THE HIGH SCHOOL, 1956				x
SPECIAL COMMITTEE ON CAMPUS TENSIONS, 1970			x	
ASSEMBLY ON UNIVERSITY GOALS AND GOVERNANCE, 1971			x	
COMMISSION ON ACADEMIC TENURE, 1973	x			
COMMISSION ON NON-TRADITIONAL STUDY, 1973			x	
COMMISSION ON CIVIL DISORDERS, 1968			x	
COMMISSION ON CAMPUS UNREST, 1970			x	
U.S. OFFICE OF EDUCATION TASK FORCE, 1971			x	
WHITE HOUSE CONFERENCE, 1971				x
CARNEGIE COMMISSION, 1973				x

TABLE C-3 "Trustees should be actively involved in the governance of institutions of higher education, including broad educational policy."

	NOT CONSIDERED	STRONG OR MODERATE OPPOSITION	MODERATE ENDORSEMENT	STRONG, POSITIVE EMPHASIS
COMMISSION ON HIGHER EDUCATION, 1947			x	
COMMISSION ON FINANCING HIGHER EDUCATION, 1952			x	
COMMITTEE ON EDUCATION BEYOND THE HIGH SCHOOL, 1956			x	
SPECIAL COMMITTEE ON CAMPUS TENSIONS, 1970				x
ASSEMBLY ON UNIVERSITY GOALS AND GOVERNANCE, 1971			x	
COMMISSION ON ACADEMIC TENURE, 1973			x	
COMMISSION ON NON-TRADITIONAL STUDY, 1973	x			
COMMISSION ON CIVIL DISORDERS, 1968	x			
COMMISSION ON CAMPUS UNREST, 1970				x
U.S. OFFICE OF EDUCATION TASK FORCE, 1971			x	
WHITE HOUSE CONFERENCE, 1971				x
CARNEGIE COMMISSION, 1973			x	

TABLE C-4 "Colleges and universities must devise ways to conserve scarce resources."

	NOT CON- SIDERED	STRONG OR MODERATE OPPOSI- TION	MODERATE ENDORSE- MENT	STRONG, POSITIVE EMPHASIS
COMMISSION ON HIGHER EDUCATION, 1947			X	
COMMISSION ON FINANCING HIGHER EDUCATION, 1952				X
COMMITTEE ON EDUCATION BEYOND THE HIGH SCHOOL, 1956			X	
SPECIAL COMMITTEE ON CAMPUS TENSIONS, 1970			X	
ASSEMBLY ON UNIVERSITY GOALS AND GOVERNANCE, 1971				X
COMMISSION ON ACADEMIC TENURE, 1973	X			
COMMISSION ON NON-TRADITIONAL STUDY, 1973	X			
COMMISSION ON CIVIL DISORDERS, 1968	X			
COMMISSION ON CAMPUS UNREST, 1970	X			
U.S. OFFICE OF EDUCATION TASK FORCE, 1971			X	
WHITE HOUSE CONFERENCE, 1971	X			
CARNEGIE COMMISSION, 1973				X

TABLE C-5 "Independence and diversity in higher education ought to be preserved."

	NOT CON- SIDERED	STRONG OR MODERATE OPPOSI— TION	MODERATE ENDORSE— MENT	STRONG, POSITIVE EMPHASIS
COMMISSION ON HIGHER EDUCATION, 1947			X	
COMMISSION ON FINANCING HIGHER EDUCATION, 1952				X
COMMITTEE ON EDUCATION BEYOND THE HIGH SCHOOL, 1956			X	
SPECIAL COMMITTEE ON CAMPUS TENSIONS, 1970	X			
ASSEMBLY ON UNIVERSITY GOALS AND GOVERNANCE, 1971				X
COMMISSION ON ACADEMIC TENURE, 1973	X			
COMMISSION ON NON-TRADITIONAL STUDY, 1973				X
COMMISSION ON CIVIL DISORDERS, 1968	X			
COMMISSION ON CAMPUS UNREST, 1970	X			
U.S. OFFICE OF EDUCATION TASK FORCE, 1971				X
WHITE HOUSE CONFERENCE, 1971	X			
CARNEGIE COMMISSION, 1973				X

TABLE C-6 "Administrators should provide more educational leadership."

	NOT CON- SIDERED	STRONG OR MODERATE OPPOSI- TION	MODERATE ENDORSE- MENT	STRONG, POSITIVE EMPHASIS
COMMISSION ON HIGHER EDUCATION, 1947			X	
COMMISSION ON FINANCING HIGHER EDUCATION, 1952			X	
COMMITTEE ON EDUCATION BEYOND THE HIGH SCHOOL, 1956			X	
SPECIAL COMMITTEE ON CAMPUS TENSIONS, 1970			X	
ASSEMBLY ON UNIVERSITY GOALS AND GOVERNANCE, 1971				X
COMMISSION ON ACADEMIC TENURE, 1973			X	
COMMISSION ON NON-TRADITIONAL STUDY, 1973	X			
COMMISSION ON CIVIL DISORDERS, 1968	X			
COMMISSION ON CAMPUS UNREST, 1970			X	
U.S. OFFICE OF EDUCATION TASK FORCE, 1971			X	
WHITE HOUSE CONFERENCE, 1971	X			
CARNEGIE COMMISSION, 1973				X

TABLE C-7 "The faculty holds the prime responsibility for self-discipline, for curricular matters, and for faculty appointments and promotions."

	NOT CON-SIDERED	STRONG OR MODERATE OPPOSI-TION	MODERATE ENDORSE-MENT	STRONG, POSITIVE EMPHASIS
COMMISSION ON HIGHER EDUCATION, 1947			X	
COMMISSION ON FINANCING HIGHER EDUCATION, 1952			X	
COMMITTEE ON EDUCATION BEYOND THE HIGH SCHOOL, 1956			X	
SPECIAL COMMITTEE ON CAMPUS TENSIONS, 1970				X
ASSEMBLY ON UNIVERSITY GOALS AND GOVERNANCE, 1971				X
COMMISSION ON ACADEMIC TENURE, 1973				X
COMMISSION ON NON-TRADITIONAL STUDY, 1973			X	
COMMISSION ON CIVIL DISORDERS, 1968	X			
COMMISSION ON CAMPUS UNREST, 1970			X	
U.S. OFFICE OF EDUCATION TASK FORCE, 1971			X	
WHITE HOUSE CONFERENCE, 1971			X	
CARNEGIE COMMISSION, 1973				X

TABLE C-8   "The tenure system should be retained unchanged."

	NOT CON- SIDERED	STRONG OR MODERATE OPPOSI- TION	MODERATE ENDORSE- MENT	STRONG, POSITIVE EMPHASIS
COMMISSION ON HIGHER EDUCATION, 1947		x		
COMMISSION ON FINANCING HIGHER EDUCATION, 1952	x			
COMMITTEE ON EDUCATION BEYOND THE HIGH SCHOOL, 1956	x			
SPECIAL COMMITTEE ON CAMPUS TENSIONS, 1970		x		
ASSEMBLY ON UNIVERSITY GOALS AND GOVERNANCE, 1971		x		
COMMISSION ON ACADEMIC TENURE, 1973		x		
COMMISSION ON NON-TRADITIONAL STUDY, 1973	x			
COMMISSION ON CIVIL DISORDERS, 1968	x			
COMMISSION ON CAMPUS UNREST, 1970		x		
U.S. OFFICE OF EDUCATION TASK FORCE, 1971		x		
WHITE HOUSE CONFERENCE, 1971		x		
CARNEGIE COMMISSION, 1973		x		

TABLE C-9 "Students should actively participate in the decision-making process related to academic matters."

	NOT CON-SIDERED	STRONG OR MODERATE OPPOSI-TION	MODERATE ENDORSE-MENT	STRONG, POSITIVE EMPHASIS
COMMISSION ON HIGHER EDUCATION, 1947				X
COMMISSION ON FINANCING HIGHER EDUCATION, 1952		X		
COMMITTEE ON EDUCATION BEYOND THE HIGH SCHOOL, 1956		X		
SPECIAL COMMITTEE ON CAMPUS TENSIONS, 1970				X
ASSEMBLY ON UNIVERSITY GOALS AND GOVERNANCE, 1971			X	
COMMISSION ON ACADEMIC TENURE, 1973			X	
COMMISSION ON NON-TRADITIONAL STUDY, 1973	X			
COMMISSION ON CIVIL DISORDERS, 1968	X			
COMMISSION ON CAMPUS UNREST, 1970				X
U.S. OFFICE OF EDUCATION TASK FORCE, 1971	X			
WHITE HOUSE CONFERENCE, 1971				X
CARNEGIE COMMISSION, 1973				X

TABLE C-10 "Federal financial assistance for higher education should be granted primarily through students rather than through institutions."

	NOT CON-SIDERED	STRONG OR MODERATE OPPOSI-TION	MODERATE ENDORSE-MENT	STRONG, POSITIVE EMPHASIS
COMMISSION ON HIGHER EDUCATION, 1947				X
COMMISSION ON FINANCING HIGHER EDUCATION, 1952		X		
COMMITTEE ON EDUCATION BEYOND THE HIGH SCHOOL, 1956			X	
SPECIAL COMMITTEE ON CAMPUS TENSIONS, 1970	X			
ASSEMBLY ON UNIVERSITY GOALS AND GOVERNANCE, 1971	X			
COMMISSION ON ACADEMIC TENURE, 1973	X			
COMMISSION ON NON-TRADITIONAL STUDY, 1973			X	
COMMISSION ON CIVIL DISORDERS, 1968			X	
COMMISSION ON CAMPUS UNREST, 1970			X	
U.S. OFFICE OF EDUCATION TASK FORCE, 1971				X
WHITE HOUSE CONFERENCE, 1971			X	
CARNEGIE COMMISSION, 1973				X

TABLE C-11   "The states should retain the major responsibility for higher education."

	NOT CON- SIDERED	STRONG OR MODERATE OPPOSI- TION	MODERATE ENDORSE- MENT	STRONG, POSITIVE EMPHASIS
COMMISSION ON HIGHER EDUCATION, 1947				X
COMMISSION ON FINANCING HIGHER EDUCATION, 1952			X	
COMMITTEE ON EDUCATION BEYOND THE HIGH SCHOOL, 1956			X	
SPECIAL COMMITTEE ON CAMPUS TENSIONS, 1970	X			
ASSEMBLY ON UNIVERSITY GOALS AND GOVERNANCE, 1971	X			
COMMISSION ON ACADEMIC TENURE, 1973	X			
COMMISSION ON NON-TRADITIONAL STUDY, 1973	X			
COMMISSION ON CIVIL DISORDERS, 1968			X	
COMMISSION ON CAMPUS UNREST, 1970	X			
U.S. OFFICE OF EDUCATION TASK FORCE, 1971			X	
WHITE HOUSE CONFERENCE, 1971	X			
CARNEGIE COMMISSION, 1973				X

TABLE C-12 "The states should initiate or increase support for private higher education."

	NOT CON-SIDERED	STRONG OR MODERATE OPPOSI-TION	MODERATE ENDORSE-MENT	STRONG, POSITIVE EMPHASIS
COMMISSION ON HIGHER EDUCATION, 1947		x		
COMMISSION ON FINANCING HIGHER EDUCATION, 1952			x	
COMMITTEE ON EDUCATION BEYOND THE HIGH SCHOOL, 1956	x			
SPECIAL COMMITTEE ON CAMPUS TENSIONS, 1970	x			
ASSEMBLY ON UNIVERSITY GOALS AND GOVERNANCE, 1971			x	
COMMISSION ON ACADEMIC TENURE, 1973	x			
COMMISSION ON NON-TRADITIONAL STUDY, 1973	x			
COMMISSION ON CIVIL DISORDERS, 1968	x			
COMMISSION ON CAMPUS UNREST, 1970	x			
U.S. OFFICE OF EDUCATION TASK FORCE, 1971			x	
WHITE HOUSE CONFERENCE, 1971	x			
CARNEGIE COMMISSION, 1973				x

APPENDIX TABLES AND CHARTS

APPENDIX TABLE 1　How the confidence ranking of major institutions has changed (in percentages)

INSTITUTIONS	1966	1971	DECLINE
TELEVISION	25	22	—12
MEDICINE	72	61	—15
MENTAL HEALTH & PSYCHIATRY	51	35	—31
ORGANIZED RELIGION	41	27	—34
ORGANIZED LABOR	22	14	—36
THE PRESS	29	18	—38
ADVERTISING	21	13	—38
EDUCATION	61	37	—39
SCIENTISTS	56	32	—43
FEDERAL EXECUTIVE BRANCH	41	23	—44
BANKS AND FINANCIAL INSTITUTIONS	67	36	—46
LOCAL RETAILERS	48	24	—50
MAJOR COMPANIES	55	27	—51
U.S. SUPREME COURT	51	23	—55
MILITARY	62	27	—56

SOURCE:　Harris Survey, Nov. 4, 1971. © The Chicago Tribune.

APPENDIX TABLE 2   Selected measures of educational attainment of the population 25 years old and over, 1910 to 1970, with Current Population Survey (CPS) and Carnegie Commission projections to the year 2000

YEAR	MEDIAN YEARS COMPLETED	PERCENTAGE WHOSE HIGHEST YEAR COMPLETED WAS			
		FOUR OF HIGH SCHOOL OR MORE	FOUR OF HIGH SCHOOL	ONE TO THREE OF COLLEGE	FOUR OR MORE OF COLLEGE
1910	8.1	13.5	n.a.*	n.a.	2.7
1920	8.2	16.4	n.a.	n.a.	3.3
1930	8.4	19.1	n.a.	n.a.	3.9
1940	8.6	24.1	14.1	5.4	4.6
1950	9.3	33.3	20.2	7.1	6.0
1960	10.6	41.1	24.6	8.8	7.7
1970	12.1	52.4	31.1	10.6	10.7
1980					
(CPS SERIES 1)	12.4	65.4	37.9	12.5	15.0
(CARNEGIE)	12.4	64.7	37.7	12.4	14.6
1990					
(CPS SERIES 1)	12.6	74.2	39.3	14.8	20.1
(CARNEGIE)	12.6	72.6	39.5	14.9	18.1
2000					
(CARNEGIE)	12.8	79.7	40.5	17.4	21.8

* n.a. = not available.

NOTE: Detail may not add to total because of rounding.

SOURCE: Prepared by John Shea of the Carnegie Commission staff, from Bureau of the Census and Carnegie Commission on Higher Education materials and assumptions.

APPENDIX CHART 1   Selected measures of educational attainment of
the population 25 to 29 years of age, 1940–2000

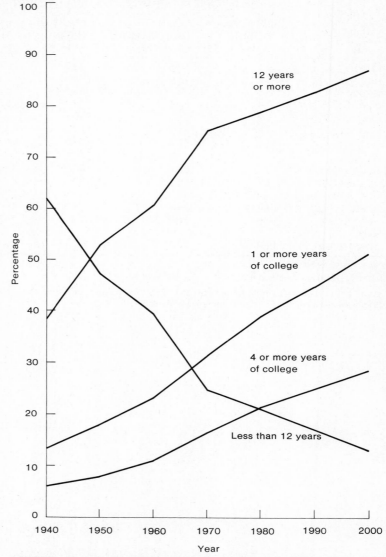

SOURCE: Carnegie Commission staff, 1973, based on Bureau of the Census
and Carnegie Commission materials and assumptions.

APPENDIX TABLE 3 Percentage of high school graduates going to college the following year, by academic aptitude, socioeconomic background, and sex, 1957, 1961, and 1967

SOCIOECONOMIC QUARTILE AND ABILITY QUARTILE	MEN				WOMEN			
				INCREASE				INCREASE
	1957	1961	1967	1961–1967	1957	1961	1967	1961–1967
1 (LOW) SOCIOECONOMIC QUARTILE								
1 (LOW) ABILITY QUARTILE	6	9	33	+24	4	8	25	+17
2	17	16	43	+27	6	13	28	+15
3	28	32	60	+28	9	25	44	+19
4 (HIGH)	52	58	75	+17	28	34	60	+26
2 SOCIOECONOMIC QUARTILE								
1 (LOW) ABILITY QUARTILE	12	14	30	+16	9	12	28	+16
2	27	25	39	+14	20	12	36	+24
3	43	38	69	+31	24	30	48	+18
4 (HIGH)	59	74	80	+ 6	37	51	73	+22
3 SOCIOECONOMIC QUARTILE								
1 (LOW) ABILITY QUARTILE	18	16	29	+13	16	13	36	+23
2	34	36	55	+19	26	21	50	+29
3	51	48	68	+20	31	40	68	+28
4 (HIGH)	72	79	89	+10	48	71	83	+12
4 (HIGH) SOCIOECONOMIC QUARTILE								
1 (LOW) ABILITY QUARTILE	39	34	57	+23	33	26	37	+11
2	61	45	61	+16	44	37	67	+30
3	73	72	79	+ 7	67	65	77	+12
4 (HIGH)	91	90	92	+ 2	76	85	93	+ 8

SOURCE: Adapted from table in K. P. Cross, *Beyond the Open Door: New Students to Higher Education*, Jossey-Bass, Inc., San Francisco, 1971, p. 7.

APPENDIX TABLE 4   Deficiencies in higher education, by state, as estimated by the Carnegie Commission as of the dates shown

	NUMBER OF OF NEW COMMUNITY COLLEGES NEEDED BY 1980 (AS OF 1970)	NUMBER OF NEW COMPREHENSIVE COLLEGES NEEDED BY 1980 (AS OF 1970)	NEW UNIVERSITY HEALTH SCIENCE CENTERS RECOMMENDED (AS OF 1970)	NUMBER OF AREA HEALTH EDUCATION CENTERS SUGGESTED (AS OF 1970)
ALABAMA	2–3			3
ALASKA				2
ARIZONA	4–5	4–5	Phoenix	1
ARKANSAS	6–7	1		2
CALIFORNIA	20–25	10–12	Fresno	10
COLORADO	5–6	2–3		2
CONNECTICUT	1–2	4–5		2
DELAWARE	2–3	1	Wilmington	
DISTRICT OF COLUMBIA				
FLORIDA	9–12	5–6	Jacksonville	1
GEORGIA	4–5	1		3
HAWAII		1		1
IDAHO	3–4	4–5		2
ILLINOIS	4–6	4		2
INDIANA	7–8	3–4		5
IOWA	3–4	1		3
KANSAS		2–3	Wichita	3
KENTUCKY	2–3	1–2		2
LOUISIANA	3–4			1
MAINE	4–5			3
MARYLAND	3–4			2
MASSACHUSETTS	6–8		Springfield	1
MICHIGAN	6–7	3–4		6
MINNESOTA	3–4	2–3	Duluth-Superior	1
MISSISSIPPI	2–3			3
MISSOURI	2–3	2–3		1
MONTANA	2–3			3
NEBRASKA	1–2	1		3
NEVADA	1–2			1
NEW HAMPSHIRE	2–3			2
NEW JERSEY	5–8	3–4		4
NEW MEXICO	3–4	4–6		2
NEW YORK	8–10			3
NORTH CAROLINA				3
NORTH DAKOTA	2–3			2
OHIO	10–14	8		5
OKLAHOMA	3–4	1	Tulsa	2
OREGON	3–4	1		2

LESS THAN 70% OF HIGH SCHOOL STUDENTS GRADUATE FROM HIGH SCHOOL (AS OF 1969)	LESS THAN 30 PLACES IN HIGHER EDUCATION INSTITUTIONS FOR EVERY 100 PERSONS IN 18–21 AGE GROUP (AS OF 1968)	LESS THAN 0.6% OF PERSONAL INCOME SPENT THROUGH LOCAL AND STATE TAXES FOR HIGHER EDUCATION (AS OF 1967–68)
X		
	X	
		X
		X
X	X	
X		
X		
		X
		X
X		
	X	
		X
		X
X		
		X

APPENDIX TABLE 4 (continued)

	NUMBER OF OF NEW COMMUNITY COLLEGES NEEDED BY 1980 (AS OF 1970)	NUMBER OF NEW COMPREHENSIVE COLLEGES NEEDED BY 1980 (AS OF 1970)	NEW UNIVERSITY HEALTH SCIENCE CENTERS RECOMMENDED (AS OF 1970)	NUMBER OF AREA HEALTH EDUCATION CENTERS SUGGESTED (AS OF 1970)
PENNSYLVANIA	6–7	4–6		7
RHODE ISLAND	2–3			
SOUTH CAROLINA				2
SOUTH DAKOTA	3–4			2
TENNESSEE	4–5	1		2
TEXAS	5–7	4		6
UTAH	3–4	2–3		1
VERMONT	3–4			1
VIRGINIA	2–4		Norfolk–Portsmouth	1
WASHINGTON	2–3	1–2		3
WEST VIRGINIA	2–3			2
WISCONSIN	1–2	1–2		3
WYOMING				2
50 STATES AND THE DISTRICT OF COLUMBIA	174–234	82–103	9	
				126
				Puerto Rico
				2

SOURCES: *The Capitol and the Campus: State Responsibility for Postsecondary Education.* A Report and Recommendations by the Carnegie Commission on Higher Education, McGraw-Hill Book Company, New York, April 1971; *Higher Education and the Nation's Health: Policies for Medical and Dental Education.* A Special Report and Recommendations by the Carnegie Commission on Higher Education, McGraw-Hill Book Company, New York, October 1970; and *New Students and New Places: Policies for the Future Growth and Development of American Higher Education.* A Report and Recommendations by the Carnegie Commission on Higher Education, McGraw-Hill Book Company, New York, October 1971.

LESS THAN 70% OF HIGH SCHOOL STUDENTS GRADUATE FROM HIGH SCHOOL (AS OF 1969)	LESS THAN 30 PLACES IN HIGHER EDUCATION INSTITUTIONS FOR EVERY 100 PERSONS IN 18–21 AGE GROUP (AS OF 1968)	LESS THAN 0.6% OF PERSONAL INCOME SPENT THROUGH LOCAL AND STATE TAXES FOR HIGHER EDUCATION (AS OF 1967–68)
		X
	X	
	X	X
6	5	9

APPENDIX TABLE 5   Deficiencies in central cities and metropolitan areas, as estimated by the Carnegie Commission as of the dates shown

	NUMBER OF NEW COMMUNITY COLLEGES NEEDED BY 1980 (AS OF DECEMBER 1972)	NUMBER OF NEW COMPREHENSIVE COLLEGES NEEDED BY 1980 (AS OF DECEMBER 1972)	HAS FEWER THAN 2.5 STUDENT PLACES PER 100 POPULATION (AS OF 1970)	DEFICIENT IN OPEN-ADMISSIONS PLACES IN CENTRAL CITY (AS OF DECEMBER 1972)
NEW ENGLAND STATES				
CONNECTICUT				
BRIDGEPORT		1		
HARTFORD	1	1		
NEW HAVEN		1		
MASSACHUSETTS				
BOSTON	2–3			
SPRINGFIELD	1			
WORCESTER	1–2			
RHODE ISLAND				
PROVIDENCE	1–2			
NORTH ATLANTIC STATES				
DISTRICT OF COLUMBIA				
METROPOLITAN AREA	3–5			
MARYLAND				
BALTIMORE	1–2			
NEW JERSEY				
JERSEY CITY	2–3	1		X
NEWARK	2–3	1		X
PATERSON-CLIFTON-PASSAIC	2	1–2	2.23	X
NEW YORK				
ALBANY-SCHENECTADY-TROY	1	1		
BUFFALO	1			
NEW YORK CITY	4–5	3–4		
ROCHESTER	1–2			
SYRACUSE	1	1		
PENNSYLVANIA				
ALLENTOWN-BETHLEHEM-EASTON (NJ)		1		
LANCASTER				X
PHILADELPHIA	2–3	2–3		X
PITTSBURGH	1	1–2		X
NORTH MIDWEST STATES				
ILLINOIS				
CHICAGO	3–4	2–3		

APPENDIX TABLE 5 (continued)

	NUMBER OF NEW COMMUNITY COLLEGES NEEDED BY 1980 (AS OF DECEMBER 1972)	NUMBER OF NEW COMPREHENSIVE COLLEGES NEEDED BY 1980 (AS OF DECEMBER 1972)	HAS FEWER THAN 2.5 STUDENT PLACES PER 100 POPULATION (AS OF 1970)	DEFICIENT IN OPEN-ADMISSIONS PLACES IN CENTRAL CITY (AS OF DECEMBER 1972)
PEORIA				X
INDIANA				
GARY–HAMMOND–				
EAST CHICAGO	1	1	2.43	
INDIANAPOLIS	1–2	2	2.12	
MICHIGAN				
DETROIT	2–3	1–2		
GRAND RAPIDS	1–2	1		
OHIO				
AKRON	1–2			
CANTON			1.52	
CINCINNATI	1–2	2		X
CLEVELAND	1–2	1		
COLUMBUS	1	1		
DAYTON	1	1		
TOLEDO	1–2	1		
YOUNGSTOWN–				
WARREN	1	1		X
WISCONSIN				
MILWAUKEE	1–2	1–2		
CENTRAL STATES				
IOWA				
DAVENPORT–ROCK				
ISLAND–MOLINE			2.47	
MINNESOTA				
MINNEAPOLIS–				
ST. PAUL		1–2		
MISSOURI				
KANSAS CITY	1	1	2.35	
ST. LOUIS	1–2	1–2		
NEBRASKA				
OMAHA	1			
SOUTHEAST STATES				
ALABAMA				
BIRMINGHAM	1			
MOBILE			2.28	
ARKANSAS				
LITTLE ROCK–NO.				
LITTLE ROCK			1.89	X
FLORIDA				

APPENDIX TABLE 5 (continued)

	NUMBER OF NEW COMMUNITY COLLEGES NEEDED BY 1980 (AS OF DECEMBER 1972)	NUMBER OF NEW COMPREHENSIVE COLLEGES NEEDED BY 1980 (AS OF DECEMBER 1972)	HAS FEWER THAN 2.5 STUDENT PLACES PER 100 POPULATION (AS OF 1970)	DEFICIENT IN OPEN-ADMISSIONS PLACES IN CENTRAL CITY (AS OF DECEMBER 1972)
FORT LAUDERDALE–HOLLYWOOD	1–2	1	1.30	
JACKSONVILLE	1–2	1*	2.32	
MIAMI	2–3	1*		
TAMPA–ST. PETERSBURG	1–2			
GEORGIA				
ATLANTA	1–2	1		X
KENTUCKY				
LOUISVILLE	1–2	1	1.93	X
LOUISIANA				
NEW ORLEANS	1–2	1		
NORTH CAROLINA				
GREENSBORO–WINSTON-SALEM–HIGH POINT	1			X
TENNESSEE				
KNOXVILLE				X
MEMPHIS	1–2	1		
NASHVILLE	1			X
VIRGINIA				
NORFOLK-PORTSMOUTH	1–2		1.85	
RICHMOND	1–2			
SOUTHWEST STATES				
ARIZONA				
PHOENIX	1–2	1		
OKLAHOMA				
OKLAHOMA CITY	1	1		
TULSA			1.69	X
TEXAS				
BEAUMONT–PORT ARTHUR–ORANGE				X
DALLAS	1	1		
EL PASO				X
FORT WORTH	1–2			
HOUSTON	2–3	1		X
SAN ANTONIO	1	1		

APPENDIX TABLE 5 (continued)

	NUMBER OF NEW COMMUNITY COLLEGES NEEDED BY 1980 (AS OF DECEMBER 1972)	NUMBER OF NEW COMPREHENSIVE COLLEGES NEEDED BY 1980 (AS OF DECEMBER 1972)	HAS FEWER THAN 2.5 STUDENT PLACES PER 100 POPULATION (AS OF 1970)	DEFICIENT IN OPEN-ADMISSIONS PLACES IN CENTRAL CITY (AS OF DECEMBER 1972)
MOUNTAIN STATES				
COLORADO				
DENVER	1–2			X
UTAH				
SALT LAKE CITY	1	1		
PACIFIC STATES				
CALIFORNIA				
ANAHEIM–SANTA ANA–				
GARDEN GROVE	2–3	1		
LOS ANGELES–LONG				
BEACH	2–4	2–3		
SACRAMENTO	1–2	1		
SAN BERNADINO	2–3	1		
SAN DIEGO	1–2	1		
SAN FRANCISCO–				
OAKLAND	2–4	1–2		
SAN JOSE	2–3	1		
HAWAII				
HONOLULU	1	1		
OREGON				
PORTLAND	1–2	1		
WASHINGTON				
SEATTLE-EVERETT	1–2	1		
TOTAL NEEDS	84–130	58–69	13 areas	20 cities

*A new university that could serve as a comprehensive college has been established.

SOURCE: *The Campus and the City: Maximizing Assets and Reducing Liabilities.* A Report and Recommendations by the Carnegie Commission on Higher Education, McGraw-Hill Book Company, New York, December 1972.

APPENDIX TABLE 6   State and local expenditure on higher education, including student aid, as a percentage of personal income

YEAR	PERCENTAGE OF PER CAPITA PERSONAL INCOME
1929–30	0.185
1931–32	
1933–34	0.203
1935–36	0.219
1937–38	0.229
1939–40	0.232
1941–42	0.177
1943–44	0.127
1945–46	0.146
1947–48	0.199
1949–50	0.254
1951–52	0.259
1953–54	0.290
1955–56	0.312
1957–58	0.364
1959–60	0.397
1961–62	0.444
1963–64	0.502
1965–66	0.608
1967–68	0.735
1968–69	0.765
1972–73	0.900*

* Estimated

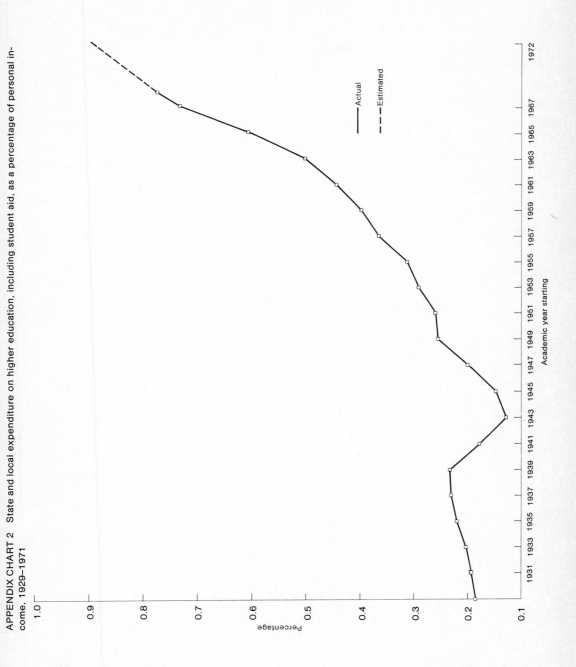

APPENDIX CHART 2   State and local expenditure on higher education, including student aid, as a percentage of personal income, 1929–1971

CARNEGIE COMMISSION REPORTS, IN CHRONOLOGICAL ORDER

APPENDIX

A

CARNEGIE COMMISSION SPONSORED STUDIES, TECHNICAL REPORTS, AND REPRINTS

APPENDIX B

SPONSORED STUDIES

1 Howard R. Bowen, *The Finance of Higher Education,* August 1968

2 William G. Bowen, *The Economics of the Major Private Universities,* August 1968

3 Ronald A. Wolk, *Alternative Methods of Federal Funding for Higher Education,* December 1968

4 Dale M. Heckman and Warren Bryan Martin, *Inventory of Current Research on Higher Education, 1968,* December 1968

5 E. Alden Dunham, *Colleges of the Forgotten Americans: A Profile of State Colleges and Regional Universities,* November 1969

6 Andrew M. Greeley, *From Backwater to Mainstream: A Profile of Catholic Higher Education,* November 1969

7 Heinz Eulau and Harold Quinley, *State Officials and Higher Education: A Survey of the Opinions and Expectations of Policy Makers in Nine States,* May 1970

8 Stephen H. Spurr, *Academic Degree Structures: Innovative Approaches—Principles of Reform in Degree Structures in the United States,* May 1970

9 Dwight R. Ladd, *Change in Educational Policy: Self-Studies in Selected Colleges and Universities,* July 1970

10 Lewis B. Mayhew, *Graduate and Professional Education, 1980: A Survey of Institutional Plans,* August 1970

11 Oscar Handlin and Mary F. Handlin, *The American College and American Culture: Socialization as a Function of Higher Education,* September 1970

12 Joe L. Spaeth and Andrew M. Greeley, *Recent Alumni and Higher Education: A Survey of College Graduates,* September 1970

13 Irwin T. Sanders and Jennifer C. Ward, *Bridges to Understanding: International Programs of American Colleges and Universities,* December 1970

14 Barbara B. Burn, with chapters by Clark Kerr, Philip Altbach, and James A. Perkins, *Higher Education in Nine Countries: A Comparative Study of Colleges and Universities Abroad,* February 1971

15 Rashi Fein and Gerald Weber, *Financing Medical Education: An Analysis of Alternative Policies and Mechanisms,* February 1971

16 Earl Cheit, *The New Depression in Higher Education,* February 1971

17 Leland L. Medsker and Dale Tillery, *Breaking the Access Barriers: A Profile of Two-Year Colleges,* March 1971

18 Frank Bowles and Frank A. DeCosta, *Between Two Worlds: A Profile of Negro Higher Education,* April 1971

19 Eric Ashby, *Any Person, Any Study: An Essay on American Higher Education,* April 1971

20 Morris Keeton, *Models and Mavericks: A Profile of the Private Liberal Arts Colleges,* May 1971

21 Robert Hartman, *Credit for College: Public Policy for Student Loans,* June 1971

22 Howard R. Bowen and Gordon K. Douglass, *Efficiency in Liberal Education: A Study of Comparative Instructional Costs for Different Ways of Organizing Teaching-Learning in a Liberal Arts College,* September 1971

23 Eugene C. Lee and Frank M. Bowen, *The Multicampus University: A Study of Academic Governance,* September 1971

24 Harold L. Hodgkinson, *Institutions in Transition: A Profile of Change in Higher Education* (incorporating the 1970 statistical report), September 1971

25 Stephen B. Withey et al, *A Degree and What Else? Correlates and Consequences of a College Education,* October 1971

26 Joseph Ben-David, *American Higher Education: Directions Old and New,* December 1971

27 Alexander W. Astin and Calvin B. T. Lee, *The Invisible Colleges: A Profile of Small, Private Colleges with Limited Resources,* January 1972

28 Harold Orlans, *The Nonprofit Research Institute: Its Origin, Operation, Problems, and Prospects,* March 1972

29 Edgar H. Schein, *Professional Education: Some New Directions,* March 1972

30 C. Robert Pace, *Education and Evangelism: A Profile of Protestant Colleges,* June 1972

31 Dael Wolfle, *The Home of Science: The Role of the University,* June 1972

32 Seymour E. Harris, *A Statistical Portrait of Higher Education,* June 1972

33 Roger E. Levien, *The Emerging Technology: Instructional Uses of the Computer in Higher Education,* November 1972

34 C. Arnold Anderson, Mary Jean Bowman, and Vincent Tinto, *Where Colleges Are and Who Attends: Effects of Accessibility on College Attendance,* November 1972

35 Herbert L. Packer and Thomas Ehrlich, *New Directions in Legal Education,* November 1972 [abridged paperback edition, April 1973]

36 James A. Perkins, *The University as an Organization,* February 1973

37 Richard Storr, *The Beginning of the Future: A Historical Approach to Graduate Education in the Arts and Sciences,* June 1973

38 David Riesman and Verne Stadtman, eds., *Academic Transformation: Seventeen Institutions Under Pressure,* June 1973

39 George Nash, *The University and the City: Eight Cases of Involvement,* June 1973

40 Jack Morrison, *The Rise of the Arts on the American Campus,* July 1973

41 Alexander Mood, *The Future of Higher Education: Some Speculations and Suggestions,* September 1973

42 Carl Kaysen, ed., *Content and Context: Essays on College Education,* October 1973

43 Alain Touraine, *The Academic System in American Society,* November 1973

44 Michael Cohen and James March, *Leadership and Ambiguity: The American College President,* November 1973

45 Stephen Steinberg, *The Academic Melting Pot: Catholics and Jews in Higher Education,* November 1973

46 Edward Gross and Paul Grambsch, *Change in University Organization: 1964–1971,* November 1973

47 Everett C. Hughes, Barrie Thorne, Agostino M. DeBaggis, Arnold Gurin, and David Williams, *Education for the Professions of Medicine, Law, Theology, and Social Welfare,* November 1973

48 Margaret S. Gordon, ed., *Higher Education and the Labor Market,* January 1974

49 Saul Feldman, *Escape from the Doll's House,* January 1974

50 Harland Bloland, *The Dissenting Academy,* forthcoming

51 Charles Bidwell, *Liberal Arts Colleges in the University,* forthcoming

52 Thomas Juster et al., *Education, Income and Human Behavior,* forthcoming

53 S. M. Lipset and David Riesman, *Essays on Harvard,* forthcoming

54 Joseph Ben-David, *Comparative Higher Education,* forthcoming

55 Roy Radner, *Econometric Models of Higher Education,* forthcoming

56 Richard Freeman, *Minority Employment Opportunities,* forthcoming

57 Everett Ladd and S. M. Lipset, *American Academics,* forthcoming

58 Florence Howe et al., *Women in Higher Education,* forthcoming

59 Earl Cheit, *The Industrial Professions,* forthcoming

60 Paul Lazarsfeld, *History of Innovations in Higher Education,* forthcoming

61 Allan Cartter, *The Ph.D. and Manpower Needs,* forthcoming

62 Martin Trow et al., *Essays on the National Survey of Higher Education,* forthcoming

63 Joseph Garbarino, *Collective Bargaining in Higher Education,* forthcoming

64 Martin Trow, *American Academics,* forthcoming

TECHNICAL REPORTS

1 Harold Hodgkinson, *Institutions in Transition: A Study of Change in Higher Education,* June 1970

2 June O'Neill, *Resource Use in Higher Education: Trends in Output and Inputs, 1930–1967,* July 1971

3 Mark S. Blumberg, *Trends and Projections of Physicians in the United States, 1967–2002,* July 1971

4 Richard E. Peterson and John A. Bilorusky, *May 1970: The Campus Aftermath of Cambodia and Kent State,* October 1971

5 Paul Taubman and Terence Wales, *Mental Ability and Higher Educational Attainment in the 20th Century,* June 1972

6   Richard E. Peterson, *American College and University Enrollment Trends in 1971,* June 1972.

7   Alexander Mood et al., *Papers on Efficiency in the Management of Higher Education,* August 1972

8   Ann Heiss, *An Inventory of Academic Innovation and Reform,* March 1973

9   Earl Cheit, *The New Depression in Higher Education—Two Years Later,* April 1973

10   Richard Eckaus, *Estimating the Returns to Education: A Disaggregated Approach,* April 1973

11   June O'Neill, *Sources of Funds to Colleges and Universities,* May 1973

12   Everett Ladd and S. M. Lipset, *Professors, Unions, and American Higher Education,* August 1973

13   Carnegie Commission on Higher Education, *Technical Notes on Purposes and Performance in Higher Education,* forthcoming

14   Michio Nagai, *Dilemmas for American Higher Education,* forthcoming

15   Carnegie Commission on Higher Education, *A Classification of Institutions of Higher Education,* forthcoming

16   Douglas Adkins, *The American Educated Labor Force: An Empirical Look at Theories of its Formation and Composition,* forthcoming

17   Margaret Fay and Jeff Weintraub, *Ideology: Crystallization, Consistency, and Context,* forthcoming

18   Thomas J. Karwin, *Flying a Learning Center: Design and Costs of an Off-Campus Base for Learning,* forthcoming

19   C. Robert Pace, *Characteristics of Institutions of Higher Education,* (working title), forthcoming

REPRINTS

1   Theodore W. Schultz, "Resources for Higher Education: An Economist's View," reprinted from *The Journal of Political Economy,* vol. 76, no. 3, May/June 1968.

2   Clark Kerr, "Industrial Relations and University Relations," reprinted from *Proceedings of the 21st Annual Winter Meeting of the Industrial Relations Research Association,* pp. 15–25.

3   Clark Kerr, "New Challenges to the College and University," reprinted from *Agenda for the Nation,* Kermit Gordon, ed., Brookings Institution, Washington, D.C., 1968.

4   Clark Kerr, "Presidential Discontent," reprinted from *Perspectives on Campus Tensions: Papers Prepared for the Special Committee on Campus Tensions,* David C. Nichols, ed., American Council on Education, Washington, D.C., September 1970.

5   Harold Hodgkinson, "Student Protest—An Institutional and National Profile," reprinted from *The Record,* vol. 71, no. 4, May 1970.

6   Kenneth Keniston, "What's Bugging the Students?" reprinted from the *Educational Record,* vol. 51, no. 2, Spring 1970.

7   Seymour M. Lipset, *The Politics of Academia,* reprinted from *Perspectives on Campus Tensions: Papers Prepared for the Special Committee on Campus Tensions,* David C. Nichols, ed., American Council on Education, Washington, D.C., September 1970.

8   Seymour M. Lipset and Everett C. Ladd, Jr., ". . . And What Professors Think," reprinted from *Psychology Today,* vol. 4, no. 6, November 1970.

9   Roy Radner and Leonard S. Miller, "Demand and Supply in U.S. Higher Education: A Progress Report," reprinted from *The American Economic Review,* vol. 60, no. 2, May 1970.

10   Kenneth Keniston and Michael Lerner, "The Unholy Alliance Against the Campus," reprinted from *The New York Times Magazine,* November 8, 1970.

11   Joseph W. Garbarino, "Precarious Professors: New Patterns of Representation," reprinted from *Industrial Relations,* vol. 10, no. 1, February 1971.

12   Earl F. Cheit, "Regent Watching," reprinted from *AGB Reports,* vol. 13, no. 6, March 1971.

13   Neil Timm, "A New Method of Measuring States' Higher Education Burden," reprinted from *The Journal of Higher Education,* vol. 42, no. 1, January 1971.

14   Seymour M. Lipset and Everett C. Ladd, Jr., "Jewish Academics in the United States: Their Achievements, Culture and Politics," reprinted from *American Jewish Year Book,* 1971.

15   Seymour M. Lipset and Everett C. Ladd, Jr., "The Divided Professoriate," reprinted from *Change,* vol. 3, no. 3, May 1971.

16 Seymour M. Lipset and Everett C. Ladd, Jr., "The Politics of American Political Scientists," reprinted from *PS,* vol. 4, no. 2, Spring 1971.

17 Allan M. Cartter, "Scientific Manpower for 1970–1985," reprinted from *Science,* vol. 172, no. 3979, April 9, 1971.

18 Seymour M. Lipset and Everett C. Ladd, Jr., "American Social Scientists and the Growth of Campus Political Activism in the 1960s" reprinted from *Social Sciences Information,* vol. 10, no. 2, April 1971.

19 Mark S. Blumberg, "Accelerated Programs of Medical Education," reprinted from *Journal of Medical Education,* vol. 46, no. 8, August 1971.

20 Seymour M. Lipset and Everett C. Ladd, Jr., "College Generations—from the 1930s to the 1960s," reprinted from *The Public Interest,* no. 25, Summer 1971.

21 James A. Perkins, "International Programs of U.S. Colleges and Universities: Priorities for the Seventies," reprinted from Occasional Paper No. 1, International Council for Educational Development, July 1971.

22 Joseph W. Garbarino, "Faculty Unionism: From Theory to Practice," reprinted from *Industrial Relations,* vol. 11, no. 1, February 1972.

23 Virginia B. Smith, "More For Less: Higher Education's New Priority," reprinted from *Universal Higher Education: Costs and Benefits,* American Council on Education, Washington, D.C., 1971.

24 Seymour M. Lipset, "Academia and Politics in America," reprinted from *Imagination and Precision in the Social Sciences,* Thomas J. Nossiter, ed., Faber and Faber, London, 1972.

25 Everett C. Ladd, Jr., and Seymour M. Lipset, "Politics of Academic Natural Scientists and Engineers," reprinted from *Science*, vol. 176, no. 4039, June 9, 1972.

26 Seymour M. Lipset and Richard B. Dobson, "The Intellectual as Critic and Rebel: With Special Reference to the United States and the Soviet Union," reprinted from *Daedalus,* vol. 101, no. 3, Summer 1972.

27 Seymour M. Lipset and Everett C. Ladd, Jr., "The Politics of American Sociologists," reprinted from *The American Journal of Sociology,* vol. 78, no. 1, July 1972.

28 Martin Trow, "The Distribution of Academic Tenure in American Higher Education," reprinted from *The Tenure Debate,* Bardwell Smith, ed., Jossey-Bass, San Francisco, 1972.

29 Alan Pifer, "The Nature and Origins of the Carnegie Commission on Higher Education," based on a speech delivered to the Pennsylvania Association of Colleges and Universities on October 16, 1972, and reprinted by permission of The Carnegie Foundation for the Advancement of Teaching.

30 Earl F. Cheit, "Coming of Middle Age in Higher Education," based on an address to the Joint Session of the American Association of State Colleges and Universities and the National Association of State Universities and Land-Grant Colleges in Washington, D.C., on November 13, 1972, and reprinted by permission of the National Association of State Universities and Land-Grant Colleges.

31 Bill Aussieker and J. W. Garbarino, "Measuring Faculty Unionism: Quantity and Quality," reprinted from *Industrial Relations,* vol. 12, no. 2, May 1973.

DATES AND LOCATIONS OF CARNEGIE COMMISSION MEETINGS, 1967–1973

APPENDIX C

DATES	LOCATION
June 1, 2, 1967	New York, New York
September 22, 23, 1967	Washington, D.C.
November 16, 17, 1967	New York, New York
January 19, 20, 1968	Chicago, Illinois
March 15, 16, 1968	Atlanta, Georgia
April 19, 20, 1968	New York, New York
June 21, 22, 1968	New York, New York
September 13, 14, 1968	New York, New York
November 15, 16, 1968	Chapel Hill, North Carolina
January 24, 25, 1969	Washington, D.C.
March 14, 15, 1969	New York, New York
June 18, 19, 20, 21, 1969	Berkeley, California
December 4, 5, 6, 1969	Washington, D.C.
February 20, 21, 1970	Boston, Massachusetts
April 17, 18, 1970	St. Louis, Missouri
June 26, 27, 1970	Urbana, Illinois
October 2, 3, 1970	Boulder, Colorado
November 6, 7, 1970	Detroit, Michigan
December 4, 5, 1970	New York, New York
January 15, 16, 1971	New Orleans, Louisiana
February 19, 20, 1971	Houston, Texas
April 16, 17, 1971	Miami Beach, Florida
June 24, 25, 26, 1971	Vancouver, British Columbia, and Seattle, Washington
October 8, 9, 1971	Philadelphia, Pennsylvania
November 5, 6, 1971	Oberlin, Ohio
December 2, 3, 4, 1971	Los Angeles, California
February 3, 4, 5, 1972	San Juan, Puerto Rico
April 13, 14, 15, 1972	Nashville, Tennessee
June 22, 23, 24, 1972	Minneapolis, Minnesota

October 5, 6, 7, 1972   Iowa City, Iowa
December 6, 7, 8, 1972   Honolulu, Hawaii

March 1, 2, 3, 1973   Albuquerque, New Mexico
May 24, 25, 1973   Princeton, New Jersey

MEMBERS OF THE CARNEGIE COMMISSION STAFF, 1967–1973[1]

APPENDIX D

Terry Y. Allen, assistant editor

Gloria Copeland, executive assistant

Florence Eisemann, senior administrative assistant

Marian L. Gade, postgraduate researcher

Margaret S. Gordon, associate director

Maureen I. Kawaoka, administrative secretary

Virginia B. Smith, associate director

Verne A. Stadtman, associate director and editor

Wendy Walton, secretary

[1] All persons who served during one-half or more of the life of the Commission on either a full-time or part-time basis, with their last titles.

MEMBERS OF THE TECHNICAL ADVISORY COMMITTEE, 1967–1973

APPENDIX E

Frederick Balderston, Chairman, Center for Research in Management Sciences, University of California, Berkeley, 1969–1973.

David Blackwell, Professor of Statistics, University of California, Berkeley, 1969–1973.

Lewis Butler, Planning Coordinator, Health Policy Program; and Adjunct Professor, School of Medicine, University of California, San Francisco, 1971–1973.

Earl Cheit, Professor of Business Administration, University of California, Berkeley, 1970–1973.

Charles Hitch, President of the University of California, 1967–1969.

Eugene Lee, Director, Institute of Governmental Studies, University of California, Berkeley, 1970–1973.

Seymour Martin Lipset, Fellow, Center for Advanced Studies in the Behavioral Sciences, Stanford, California, 1972–1973.

Thomas R. McConnell, Professor of Education, Emeritus, University of California, Berkeley, 1967–1973.

Joseph Pechman, then Visiting Professor, Department of Economics, University of California, Berkeley, 1970–1971.

Roy Radner, Professor of Economics and Statistics, University of California, Berkeley, 1967–1973.

David Riesman, then Fellow, Center for Advanced Studies in the Behavioral Sciences, Stanford, California, 1968–1969.

George Shultz, then Fellow, Center for Advanced Studies in the Behavioral Sciences, Stanford, California, 1968–1969.

Neil Smelser, University Professor of Sociology, University of California, Berkeley, 1967–1973.

Martin Trow, Professor of Sociology, University of California, Berkeley, 1967–1973.

Lloyd Ulman, Director, Institute of Industrial Relations, University of California, Berkeley, 1968–1973.

THE NATURE AND ORIGINS OF THE CARNEGIE COMMISSION ON HIGHER EDUCATION

APPENDIX

F

BY ALAN PIFER, PRESIDENT
The Carnegie Foundation for the Advancement of Teaching

Based on a Speech Delivered to the Pennsylvania Association of Colleges and Universities, October 16, 1972

I must tell you how gratified I am that the Pennsylvania Association of Colleges and Universities not only devoted its annual meeting last year to the work of the Carnegie Commission on Higher Education but is doing so again today. Now perhaps this is no more than just a proper show of state pride that six of the Commission members, including the chairman, are native sons and daughters of Pennsylvania. However, I choose to think your discussions are taking place because of keen interest in the Commission's findings, and that this in turn is a form of praise for its work. If it is, and if I may be both candid and immodest, it is praise that is entirely warranted. Clark Kerr and his associates on the Commission, and its staff, have, in my view, done a superb job.

I am not going to talk today about the Carnegie Commission's recommendations. Rather, I am going to discuss and try to assess for you the nature of the Commission; its origins, its membership; its relationship to the two Carnegie foundations, to the higher educational community, and to government; its legitimacy; its schedule and activities; its achievements and shortcomings; and, finally, its impact.

Origins In 1905 The Carnegie Foundation for the Advancement of Teaching was established for the specific purpose of providing free pensions for college teachers and their widows. This was six years before the founding of Carnegie Corporation of New York, the largest and most general of the trusts, institutes, and foundations created by Andrew Carnegie. The charter of the Foundation included a much broader general purpose as well. This was "to do and perform all things necessary to encourage, uphold, and dignify the profession of the teacher and the cause of higher education in the United States. . . ." Henry Prichett, the highly able first president of the Foundation, wrote perceptively to Mr. Carnegie shortly after the founding:

> . . . the more I have seen of the work the more clearly I understand that the Foundation is to become one of the great educational influences in our country, because it is going to deal, necessarily, not alone with the payment of retirement pensions to deserving teachers, but as well with the most far-reaching educational questions, and with the most important problems of educational policy. . . .

For a number of years studies supported by the Foundation had the kind of influence that Prichett foresaw, but by 1966 the Foundation was at a low ebb and faced an uncertain future. Its pension mission was virtually fulfilled, and its future income, beyond that required for pensions, would be tied up for years to come in the repayment of some huge debts acquired at an earlier period to meet pension obligations. It had no current program of any great consequence and almost no staff of its own. There was reason to believe that the time might have come to merge the Foundation into Carnegie Corporation.

Nevertheless, after careful thought by the boards of the two foundations and their joint officers, that idea was rejected, essentially on the grounds that a foundation exclusively devoted to the welfare of higher education was sufficiently unusual in our national life to be worth preserving—provided it had sufficient free funds to accomplish something important.

The Corporation, therefore, agreed to give special consideration to a proposal from the Foundation's trustees for support of some major project or study in the field of higher education, and if this rated well in the general competition for the Corporation's grants, to fund it. The Foundation's 25 trustees, almost all of whom were college and university presidents, then came up with the idea of a study of the financing of higher education. Previous studies of this subject, they agreed, were totally out of date and a new one was much needed.

The decision to undertake the study was made at the Foundation's annual meeting on November 26, 1966, and was approved in principle, with initial funding, by the Corporation's trustees on January 19, 1967. Between those dates, specifically on December 21—and the date is important in view of subsequent events—Clark Kerr, who was then president of the University of California, accepted the invitation to be chairman of the special commission that was to make the study. The appointment was to be of a public service nature, part-time and unpaid.

In that initial discussion we had with Mr. Kerr, he made the telling point that he could see no way to study the financing of higher education without looking more broadly at its structure and functions. We agreed, and the project was then designated the Carnegie Commission to Study the Future Structure, Functions, and Financing of Higher Education, soon shortened to the Carnegie Commission on the Future of Higher Education, and not long thereafter to the Carnegie Commission on Higher Education—informally, "the Kerr Commission."

Immediately after our talk with Clark Kerr, he set off for a quick visit to Hong Kong and Vietnam. Returning to San Francisco January 7, he was interviewed by the press regarding rumors that he would resign from the California presidency over Governor Ronald Reagan's proposal to impose tuition charges upon California residents attending the university. Mr. Kerr disclaimed any intention of resigning and also denied that he was looking for another job. He simply noted that he had been "talking with The Carnegie Foundation for the Advancement of Teaching about giving some of his time to head up a survey of American universities," as he put it.

On January 20, Mr. Kerr, rather unexpectedly, was dismissed from the university presidency by the California Regents, giving him an opportunity to make his famous quip—that he entered the presidency fired with enthusiasm and left the same way! This event, however, caused the Foundation to announce the establishment of its Commission quite a bit sooner than had been planned. In making the announcement on January 24, I was able to say, and say with conviction, on behalf of the trustees and officers, "Since Mr. Kerr was invited to chair the Carnegie Commission nothing has happened to change our view that no man is better qualified than he to head a study of higher education's future in this country."

We asked him to be chairman of the Commission, as the timing of events shows, well before his dismissal by the Regents because we believed he was the best person for this role—perhaps the only person in the country who could really bring it off. His abrupt firing did, however, make it possible for him to accept on a virtually full-time basis the combined positions of chairman and executive director, and for this we will always be grateful to Governor Reagan!

Membership   Although announcement of the Commission took place earlier than expected, a list of 14 potential members of it had been drawn up and these individuals were approached in good time so that their names could be included in the announcement. They were selected for their known ability, experience, judgment, objectivity, and interest in higher education. Six of the members were trustees of the Foundation as well as being college or university presidents, one was the head of a junior college district, one was a professor, one was the head of a research institute, one was a former governor of this state, one was a publisher, and three were industrialists who were also university or college trustees.

We realized, of course, that there were omissions, but we were adamant that the Commission's independence should not in any way be compromised by the addition of individuals who would feel obliged to represent constituency positions. In time, however, the Commission itself began to feel the need for additional experience in its deliberations; five other persons were added—the deans of two predominantly black law schools, the president of a four-year state college, a professor of psychology on a medical school faculty, and a British authority on international higher education. Meanwhile, one member had resigned for health reasons, making a final membership of 19, including the chairman.

From time to time since then, the work of the Commission has come under attack from certain critics because of the nature of its membership. Being careful to identify as many Commission members as possible only by their so-called "corporate links," they have charged that anything coming out of the Commission is bound to be tainted with a big business point of view.

There are, in fact, just four Commission members, out of a total membership of 19, with business backgrounds. One of these, Norton Simon, was, and still is, a regent of the University of California; a second, Clifton Phalen, was chairman, and is still a member, of the board of trustees of the State University of New York; a third, Ralph Besse, was chairman of the Cleveland Coordinating Council for Higher Education, has been a member of a number of national and state bodies concerned with community colleges and with vocational education and is presently the chairman of the board of trustees of Case Western Reserve University; a fourth, William Scranton, while governor of Pennsylvania, showed a keen interest in the development of higher education, has been a trustee of three private universities, and was chairman of the President's Commission on Campus Unrest.

These four members were selected not as representatives of business, or of anything else, but because, as I have indicated, they had special experience in the governance of higher education and a demonstrated broad interest in the field generally. Their contribution to the Commission's work has, as we expected, been substantial and one that has been greatly appreciated and respected by their fellow members.

It is, of course, the work of the Commission as a whole, rather than the characteristics of individual members, that should be the basis of any fair and reasonable judgments about it. The essential test is whether the product is proving to be helpful to the nation in the exceedingly complex task of illuminating future paths for higher education.

Relationship to Carnegie Corporation and to The Carnegie Foundation for the Advancement of Teaching   Carnegie Corporation has, since 1967, made annual grants to The Carnegie Foundation for the Advancement of Teaching to meet most of the Commission's expenses. Since these grants now total five and two-thirds million dollars, the Corporation's role has not been negligible, although it has been indirect. The Foundation, however, sponsors the Commission. In a technical, administrative sense, the Commission is, in fact, an integral part of the Foundation. Staff members of the Commission are the Foundation's employees and the Commission's headquarters at Berkeley, California, is its West Coast office.

Yet it is also clear that the Commission was created as an independent entity, reporting not to the Foundation but to the American people. Although its operations are subject to an annual budgetary review by the Foundation, the Commission's findings are developed independently and are not subject to clearance or approval by the Foundation's or the Corporation's trustees or officers. Each Commission report carries an inscription on the flyleaf which reads:

The views and conclusions expressed in this report are solely those of the members of the Carnegie Commission on Higher Education and do not necessarily reflect the views or opinions of Carnegie Corporation of New York, The Carnegie Foundation for the Advancement of Teaching, or their trustees, officers, directors, or employees.

Relationship to Higher Education and Government   It should be evident that the Commission does not in any respect "represent" higher education, including its associations, its institutions, or its estates—that is, trustees, administrators, faculty, students, and alumni. Its mission is to speak to the nation *about* the vast enterprise of higher education, not *for* it. In no sense is it an advocate for the higher educational community, nor is it beholden to this community or answerable to it, except, of course, for the factual accuracy of the data and statements it publishes.

Just as the Commission stands in an independent position in relation to higher education, so it stands with government, both federal and state. It is a totally private activity, privately financed, and privately controlled; no public official has influenced its deliberations or its findings.

The Commission, as legally an activity of The Carnegie Foundation for the Advancement of Teaching, is, of course, subject to the regulations of the Tax Reform Act of 1969. The Act has a general prohibition against foundations' lobbying or attempting to influence the opinion of the public or of officials in a legislative matter. But in the definition of what constitutes "influencing," the Act specifically exempts "making available the results of nonpartisan analysis, study, or research." It also permits foundations to provide "technical advice or assistance to a governmental body or to a committee or other subdivision thereof in response to a written request by such body or subdivision."

The Commission's reports *have* been made widely available to appropriate officials, and the Commission, sometimes as a body and sometimes through its chairman, has responded to formal requests by both elected and appointed officials to consult with them, give evidence at hearings, provide data, and offer opinions.

The Commission's Legitimacy   Although there are some people who approve of the Commission but feel it may on occasion have been too influential with government, there are others who question its legitimacy. By what right, they ask, does a foundation, accountable only to its own board of trustees, set up a private commission to study an activity of great national importance and make public pronouncements about it that may influence the development of public policy?

The work of the Commission is not the first large-scale public inquiry initiated by one or the other of the two Carnegie foundations. At a much earlier period, the Foundation for the Advancement of Teaching organized the study by Abraham Flexner that led to the reform and modernization of medical education. Later, the Corporation commissioned the Myrdal study of the American Negro that was quite influential in the ultimate rejection of the "separate but equal" doctrine in the education of blacks. About a dozen years ago it established the Ashby Commission on postsecondary education in Nigeria, and more recently, the Carnegie Commission on Educational Television.

The Carnegie Commission on Higher Education, has, however, been the most comprehensive enterprise of this kind that either of the two foundations has ever launched, and we were bound to wonder if our right to establish it would be questioned.

In one sense, the Commission's legitimacy is not a valid issue. It has no power to act on its own; it can only, through the quality of its work, inform, enlighten, and persuade those who do have the power to act. The legitimacy of such activity is firmly rooted in the constitutional right to freedom of speech.

Beyond that, it is appropriate to note that the accountability of foundations is not just to their boards of trustees. Ultimately, because they are bodies established to operate in the public interest, they must answer to the public at large. They have an obligation to inform the public fully about what they are doing, to do their work competently, and to make their decisions with integrity and objectivity. Being private institutions, however, they are not obligated any more than a private college, voluntary hospital, or private welfare agency to submit their decisions to public authority for approval.

If the activities that foundations support ultimately affect public policy, this will be the result of their successful competition in the marketplace of ideas. The public, in other words, has a completely effective mechanism for control simply in accepting or not accepting the products of private endeavor. Thus, the public will either find what the Commission has to say helpful and convincing, or it will not. And if it does not, no matter what the length of its shelf of publications, it will have no influence whatsoever.

This, again, is one of the features of an open society such as ours. No voice has automatic authority, no words are guaranteed gospel; there will always be a multiplicity of voices and competition among them to be heard. There are, of course, many other voices besides that of the Commission speaking about higher education. Some of these agree with the Commission, some disagree; and this is as it should be.

Schedule and Activities   Once the full scope of the Commission's task had been determined, it became obvious that it would need at least five years to complete its work. As it turns out, the time needed will be six years and perhaps a bit more. The Commission is presently scheduled to publish its final report in the fall of 1973.

By that time it will have held 24 two- or three-day meetings in 22 different cities in all parts of the country. It will have issued in its own name more than 20 substantial interim reports and a final report. It will have published some 60 commissioned research reports and a half-dozen technical reports, many of these of book length. The chairman will have held at least a dozen press conferences, appeared on television several times, and spoken at countless meetings, as will have other Commissioners and staff members. All in all, the sheer volume of work accomplished by the Commission, when completed about a year from now, will be staggering.

Achievements, Shortcomings and Impact   It is far too early to attempt anything like a comprehensive evaluation of the Commission. Some of its most important reports, including the final report, are still to come, and even thereafter it will be some time before the Commission's ultimate impact becomes clear. Any effort at assessment now can therefore be only impressionistic. It must also in my case obviously be subject to some bias on the favorable side. But with those caveats, I do have some preliminary views I might share with you.

The most remarkable thing about the Commission, to me, has been its capacity to take under review the entire, vast, diffuse enterprise of American higher education in virtually all of its multifold aspects—aspects as varied as functions, structure, governance, relationship to other institutions and levels of education, demand and access, expenditure, effective use of resources, technology, and reform. Conceptually, this has been a remarkable feat. The Commission has described and analyzed higher education as this has never been done before and in the process has contributed enormously to the literature on this subject.

I have also been impressed by the general temper of the Commission's work, which, it seems to me, has been dispassionate, objective, fair-minded, factually based, and imbued with a sense of pragmatic realism. Carrying out its study in a period when higher education itself has been in a state of turmoil and the object of more public concern than ever before in its history, the Commission might easily have joined the chorus of emotional critics or die-hard defenders of the academic enterprise. But it has resisted these temptations.

I have also been pleased by the wide press coverage many of the Commission's reports have received and by evidence that they are being carefully studied by public officials concerned with higher education, by college and university trustees, by presidents and by other administrative officers. Little evidence has come to my attention that faculty members or students are reading the reports or have much interest in them, but I hope I am wrong about this.

A problem we did not foresee when we set up the Commission was the degree to which it would quickly become subject to enormous pressures, both at the state and federal levels, to provide data, offer counsel, and generally be an expert witness in regard to current problems and discussions affecting higher education. These requests have been well motivated, and it has seemed in the public interest to meet them. Nevertheless, the Commission has had its own agenda and could not allow itself to become too much diverted from this. It is my impression that Clark Kerr and his colleagues have achieved a skillful balance between responding to immediate demands and sticking to the Commission's main objective of taking a long-range look at higher education's problems and potential.

I have alluded to some of the criticisms that have been directed at the Commission. One of these, that it reflects a big business point of view, has been answered. Another, that it has at times been too influential in the formulation of public policy is, I believe, based on the false premise that it should not be influential. If the influence of a body of this kind derives from the persuasiveness of its product, as it does here, there is nothing improper in being influential. On the contrary, it should be influential.

A third criticism is that the Commission has been too much wedded to the status quo in its reports. A careful reading of these reports, especially *Less Time, More Options* and the reports on medical education, on campus reform, and on instructional technology will, I believe, refute this charge. It must be said, however, that the very calmness and coolness of the Commission's style has, perhaps, made it appear to some observers to be more of a defender of the status quo of conventional approaches than it is. And it is certainly true if "conservative" means recognizing that, whatever its faults, there is much that is good about higher education as we have developed it in this country, and recognizing also that many hundreds of thousands of faculty members, administrators and trustees involved in it are doing their very best to provide quality education at the lowest possible cost to taxpayers, parents, and students.

A more substantial question, I would say, is whether the Commission has fully come to grips with one of the most difficult and most central issues in higher education today, namely its content—particularly the content of undergraduate education, and, within that, what many regard as the "disaster area" of liberal education. It is true that some of the research studies sponsored by the Commission deal with the subject of liberal education. These include the superb commentaries by two foreign observers, Sir Eric Ashby and Joseph Ben-David, and a forthcoming book entitled *Content and Context: Essays on College Education,* edited by Carl Kaysen. It is also true that the Commission's own report, *Reform on Campus: Changing Students, Changing Academic Programs,* has a few excellent pages on the subject. Nonetheless, I think it is fair to say that the Commission has not really met the question head-on and explored it thoroughly—for good reasons, I realize, although I remain somewhat wistful that it has not done so.

Lastly, there is the question of the Commission's impact. Some of the Commission's recommendations have already been widely influential and have clearly affected the development of both public and private policies. Other recommendations have provoked extensive discussion and debate. The research by specialists and observers that the Commission has sponsored, and the work of its own chairman and staff have unquestionably increased the available knowledge about higher education substantially. Impact of this kind will be even greater before the Commission concludes its work.

Speaking for the two Carnegie foundations, I believe this is about all the impact we would want the Commission to have. Its objective was never one of devising and then gaining acceptance for some huge master plan for higher education. Its mission, rather, is to be found in the words of Carnegie Corporation's charter itself, "the advancement and diffusion of knowledge and understanding." We believe the Commission is achieving that purpose and we trust that higher education will, as a result, be stronger and better able to serve the nation's needs.

A CHANCE TO LEARN: AN ACTION AGENDA FOR EQUAL OPPORTUNITY IN HIGHER EDUCATION, MARCH 1970

THE OPEN-DOOR COLLEGES: POLICIES FOR COMMUNITY COLLEGES, JUNE 1970

HIGHER EDUCATION AND THE NATION'S HEALTH: POLICIES FOR MEDICAL AND DENTAL EDUCATION, OCTOBER 1970

LESS TIME, MORE OPTIONS: EDUCATION BEYOND THE HIGH SCHOOL, NOVEMBER 1970

FROM ISOLATION TO MAINSTREAM: PROBLEMS OF COLLEGES FOUNDED FOR NEGROES, MARCH 1971

THE CAPITOL AND THE CAMPUS: STATE RESPONSIBILITY FOR POSTSECONDARY EDUCATION, APRIL 1971

INSTITUTIONAL AID: FEDERAL SUPPORT TO COLLEGES AND UNIVERSITIES, FEBRUARY 1972

THE FOURTH REVOLUTION: INSTRUCTIONAL TECHNOLOGY IN HIGHER EDUCATION, JUNE 1972

THE MORE EFFECTIVE USE OF RESOURCES: AN IMPERATIVE FOR HIGHER EDUCATION, JUNE 1972

REFORM ON CAMPUS: CHANGING STUDENTS, CHANGING ACADEMIC PROGRAMS, JUNE 1972

THE CAMPUS AND THE CITY: MAXIMIZING ASSETS AND REDUCING LIABILITIES, DECEMBER 1972

COLLEGE GRADUATES AND JOBS: ADJUSTING TO A NEW LABOR MARKET SITUATION, APRIL 1973

GOVERNANCE OF HIGHER EDUCATION: SIX PRIORITY PROBLEMS, APRIL 1973

University of Utah: Report of the University of Utah Commission to Study Tenure (1971)   Yale University Study Commission on Governance: Final Report (1971)   American Association of Higher Education–National Education Association Task Force on Faculty Representation and Academic Negotiations: Faculty Participation in Academic Governance (1967)   American Association of State Colleges and Universities: Academic Freedom and Responsibility, and Academic Tenure (1971)   American Council on Education: Report of the Special Committee on Campus Tensions (1970) American Academy of Arts and Sciences, Assembly on University Goals and Governance: A First Report (1971)   Association of American Colleges: Statement of Financial Exigency and Staff Reduction (1971)   Great Britain: Joint Statement from the Committee of Vice Chancellors and Principals and the National Union of Students (1968)   The Report of the President's Commission on Campus Unrest (1970)   White House Conference on Youth: Task Force Recommendations, Education (1971)   Columbia University: A Plan for Participation: Proposal for a University Senate with Faculty, Student, Administration and other Membership (1969)   Ohio State University: A Proposal for the Establishment of a University Senate for The Ohio State University, as amended through April 1972   Princeton University Special Committee on the Structure of the University: A Proposal to Establish The Council of The Princeton University Community (1969)   University of Minnesota: Constitution and By-laws of the University Senate (1969) University of New Hampshire: Report of the Committee on Government Organization (1969)   The University of Toronto Act (1971)

THE PURPOSES AND THE PERFORMANCE OF HIGHER EDUCATION IN THE UNITED STATES: APPROACHING THE YEAR 2000, JUNE 1973

NOTE: A technical report presenting data related to chapters 3, 4, 5, and 6 will be printed separately and will be available directly from the Carnegie Commission on Higher Education. It will be entitled *Technical Notes on Purposes and Performance in Higher Education.*

HIGHER EDUCATION: WHO PAYS? WHO BENEFITS? WHO SHOULD PAY?, JULY 1973

CONTINUITY AND DISCONTINUITY: HIGHER EDUCATION AND THE SCHOOLS, AUGUST 1973

OPPORTUNITIES FOR WOMEN IN HIGHER EDUCATION: THEIR CURRENT PARTICIPATION, PROSPECTS FOR THE FUTURE, AND RECOMMENDATIONS FOR ACTION, SEPTEMBER 1973

TOWARD A LEARNING SOCIETY: ALTERNATIVE CHANNELS TO LIFE, WORK, AND SERVICE, OCTOBER 1973